307.7 Hanmer, Trudy
HAN
     The growth of cities

                                10104

DATE			

The Growth of Cities

Trudy Hanmer

THE GROWTH OF CITIES

*Issues in American
History*

*Franklin Watts
New York/London/Toronto
Sydney/1985*

The poem "They Will Say" from *Chicago Poems* by Carl Sandburg;
copyright 1916 by Holt, Rinehart and Winston, Inc.;
renewed 1944 by Carl Sandburg. Reprinted by permission of
Harcourt Brace Jovanovich, Inc.

Photographs courtesy of:
New York Public Library Picture Collection:
frontis, pp. 5, 100;
The Bettmann Archive:
pp. 30, 39, 45, 56, 61, 78;
UPI/Bettmann Newsphotos: p. 91;
Texas Highway Department: p. 110.

Library of Congress Cataloging in Publication Data

Hanmer, Trudy J.
The growth of cities.

(Issues in American history)
Bibliography: p.
Includes index.
Summary: Traces the growth of cities in America
from colonial days to modern times and discusses the
problems and promises of urbanization.
1. Cities and towns—United States—Growth.
2. Urbanization—United States. [1. Cities and towns—
Growth.   2. Urbanization]   I. Title.
HT371.H29   1985   307.7'64'0973   85-8781
ISBN 0-531-10056-1

Contents

The Growth of Cities

For the students of
the Emma Willard School

The Beginning:
Tradition and Innovation
in Colonial Cities

When we first begin learning about American history, the story seems to be one of wilderness, a tale of people conquering forests and plains, challenging nature to wrest productive farms from a harsh frontier. In fact, for many years people explained American history according to the "frontier theory" developed by a famous historian, Frederick Jackson Turner. Turner believed that many of the most important events and movements in the history of the United States could be explained by the continuing presence of a frontier.

As important as this "frontier theory" is to an understanding of American history, it is not the complete story. Since 1830 urbanization, the rise of the city to a position of supremacy in American life, has been an equally dominant force in American history. As Turner demonstrated in his famous theory, the wilderness as the early settlers knew it had disappeared by the census of 1890, a hundred years after the Constitution went into effect. On the other hand, cities, or at least towns, have been with us from the beginning, and urbanization is still a major theme in American life almost two hundred years after the signing of the Constitution.

One of the first acts of the Congress under the new Constitution was to order a census to count the people of the new nation and to determine the numbers of people living in communities of different sizes. For purposes of this census of 1790 any locality containing more than 2,500 people was considered to be an urban area. By this measure twenty-four places were deemed to be "cities," or "towns" as they were more likely (and more appropriately) called. In 1790 these twenty-four towns comprised only 5.1 percent of the population of the nation as a whole.

As time has passed, the definition of what an American city is, in terms of population, has changed. In 1960 the Bureau of the Census defined cities as areas with a population of fifty thousand or more and began to identify not only cities but also "urban areas," cities plus the densely populated land surrounding them. The definition of an urban area was refined even further by the census of 1980. By that year the census bureau defined an urban area as "any group of 50,000 with an average density of 1,000 per square mile."

No matter what the definition, it has been clear for more than 150 years of American life that densely populated areas of the country have been growing at a much faster rate than rural areas. By the time of the census of 1980 the nation's largest city, New York, had a population of 7,015,608, and by 1982 this population was estimated to have grown to 7,086,096. Fort Lauderdale, Florida, the nation's hundredth largest city in 1980, had almost five hundred thousand people, which is far more than the combined population of all twenty-four of the nation's cities in 1790.

Early Patterns of Urbanization
Although the definition of *city* has changed over the years, there are constants in the process of urbanization that not only help to explain American history but also provide useful comparisons between the super-cities of today and the market towns of colonial America. The idea of a large group of people being identified as a city is as old as Greco-Roman city-states and the Western tradition of civilization transplanted in the New World by British and Europeans. As a majority of the early colonists were from Great Britain, it was British

custom and tradition that most often set the patterns for the initial development of American institutions, and the institution of the city was no exception.

The walled towns of ancient Greece and Rome, the bishops' sees (distinct areas controlled by the church), and the boroughs of England had in common the fact that each one formed a political entity, governed by some form of central authority. This was true of the earliest towns in colonial Virginia and New England. The town charters given by the crown to the settlers of such early colonial cities as Boston, New York, and Philadelphia were not unlike the charters governing the cities back home in England. The purpose of these charters was control. The king retained control over his subjects by vesting in the aristocracy the power to rule over any area where a large group of people lived together.

But it is not only in their tradition of local government that cities of the modern United States share a common heritage with colonial cities and their Old World ancestors. Again following patterns established long before the voyages of Columbus, the cities of the United States were formed for a variety of common purposes—as markets and as focal points of communication and transportation. Earlier cities had once served as centers of local trade for an agricultural area. By the end of the fifteenth century, however, cities were becoming marketplaces where raw materials from distant lands were exchanged for manufactured goods. Most often this meant a location on the coast or on a navigable inland waterway.

London on the Thames, Paris on the Seine, and Albany on the Hudson made perfect sense to the seventeenth-century trapper, shipbuilder, merchant, or entrepreneur. In 1680 a colonial royal governor interpreted the king of England as "resolved as soon as store-houses and conveniences can be provided, to prohibit ships trading here [the colonies] to load or unload but at certain fixed places." Those "fixed places" would grow to be colonial cities.

Colonial Cities
Although the colonial cities served many of the same functions as the older cities of Europe and England, the pattern of their development was new and distinctly American. The cities of the Old World had developed when the growth of a farming community necessitated the development of a trading center. The opposite was true in the American colonies, where one of the first goals of the settlers was to establish an urban commu-nity. Arthur M. Schlesinger, in *The City in American History* (1940), explains that these urban areas were "to serve as a means of companionship and mutual protec-tion and as a base from which to colonize the neigh-boring country." In other words, the towns and cities in the New World were necessary jumping-off points for settlers who wished to try pioneer farming. The coastal towns of the colonies were an absolute neces-sity if the pioneer farmers were to survive, market their products, and maintain communication with the Old World. By 1730 the major colonial cities were all sea-ports. In that year the leading city, Boston, numbered thirteen thousand people, with Philadelphia in second place with eleven thousand. New York, which would overtake both cities in population in the nineteenth century, was third in 1730 with eight thousand people.

If the order of the development of colonial cities was very different from that of their British counterparts, the style of their development was not. The early colonial cities were planned communities that were laid out along

*Colonial Boston in the 1730s, when it was
the biggest city in the New World*

patterns familiar to the English citizens who designed them. These early cities were not democratic, and their street plans reflect this lack of democracy. Even in tolerant Quaker Pennsylvania, William Penn proposed that Philadelphia be a grid with five spacious squares on which the leading citizens could establish estates. Those squares were centers of aristocratic society and sources of political and economic power for the Pennsylvania colony. Other colonial cities followed this same practice. Street plans revealed society's ranks. Wide avenues for estates were set aside for the upper classes; narrower streets in less ideal locations were planned to house working people.

The American Revolution
In spite of the colonies' initial mimicry of the British system of class rank, American cities were destined to become the breeding ground of the American Revolution, a war fought, in part at least, against the rigid class structure of the Old World. Benjamin Franklin, Alexander Hamilton, John Hancock, and many other Revolutionary leaders were raised in colonial cities. These cities served as centers of colonial communication and culture. By 1776 there were seven newspapers in Philadelphia, four in Boston, and at least one in every other colonial town of any size. The revolutionary debate spread through these city papers.

The theory of the Revolution was underpinned by the reality of colonial cities that did not sustain the British class system. By the eighteenth century American cities were synonymous with material opportunity. As Carl Bridenbaugh has demonstrated in *Cities in the Wilderness*, his history of the first colonial cities, craftspeople in northern colonial cities were awarded a high degree of respectability and social mobility. Social mobility means that people who were born in one economic or social class may move to a higher position in society within their lifetimes. The same artisans who held positions of respect in the colonies had been classified as "mean or base" in England. It is no wonder then that they were willing and eager to throw off the economic chains binding them to the mother country.

For all of the inhabitants of the colonial cities the seemingly unlimited opportunity for prosperity and upward social mobility meant a growing economic ambition that made these early urbanites chafe under the restrictions of the Navigation Acts, British legislation that defined how and what goods could be imported to the colonies and exported from them. In addition, their experiences in working together in the early years to ward off threats of Indian attack and to establish local government gave them associations that could be turned readily to military advantage in time of war. Ironically, the "fixed places" ordered by the king became centers of cultural life, economic growth, and political experience that would lead to the overthrow of his control.

Early Southern Cities

At the same time that many northern colonial cities were establishing themselves as centers of trade and politics, a different pattern of urbanization was developing in the southern colonies. These colonies were far more likely to develop their few cities along the lines of the older cities of Europe, so that by 1860 it was common to speak of the rural South and the urban North. Plantations in Virginia, Georgia, and the Carolinas provided an agricultural reason for the growth of seaport cities to transport their goods to the Old World. These cities, however, did not develop as manufacturing and cultural centers as quickly as did the cities of the North. As early as 1671 a leader of the Carolinas observed the backwardness of the southern cities with respect to their northern neighbors. He urged the "Planting of People in Townes," a task he identified as the "cheife thing that hath given New England soe much the advantage over Virginia."

In part the southern reluctance to urbanize came from an early aversion to urban life that was ingrained in the white southern aristocratic culture. Southern life revolved around agrarian land ownership. Trade and commerce were scorned as "ungentlemanly" pastimes—and trade and commerce were major reasons for the existence of cities. Southerners were not alone in their ambivalence toward the city. Between 1776 and 1830 the percentage of urban-dwellers among the population of the United States grew very slowly. During that time people argued whether cities were good or bad, and it was believed that their growth could be controlled or even stopped.

The End of the Colonial Period
After 1830, however, the waves of new immigrants and the explosion of the Industrial Revolution, with its factories and machinery most often located in urban areas, added two new dynamic forces to that of urbanization. With immigration and industrialization the urbanization of America could not be stopped. From that point on, the questions about American urbanization became how to urbanize, not whether or not to urbanize.

The Puritan leader, John Winthrop, characterized Boston as "a City on a Hill" in 1630. The period between 1630 and the growth of Boston in the 1840s with a teeming Irish immigrant population marked the first chapter in the history of American urbanization. The next chapters would unfold much more rapidly, as the history of the cities determined the history of the nation in a thousand ways.

2 | *The City in American Thought: Sodom or Utopia*

When Jimmy Carter won the presidential election of 1976, he did so in large part because he was able to capture the "urban vote." That year the Carter-Mondale ticket carried all but three of the heavily populated northeastern cities. Their votes in these cities meant the difference between winning and losing the 103 electoral votes represented by the states of Maryland, New York, Ohio, and Pennsylvania. Those 103 electoral votes equaled one-third of the total vote captured by the Democratic ticket in 1976. Yet when Jimmy Carter spoke to the American people, it was most often as a small-town boy from the rural Georgia town of Plains. Newspapers featured him playing softball, going fishing, and extolling the virtues of rural life. The nation that read these newspapers and voted in the majority for Carter for president was overwhelmingly urban. Yet to be a successful candidate, Carter was advised to capitalize on his homespun, rural roots.

The Carter campaign is symbolic of a deep tension in American minds over the virtue or lack of virtue of urban life. Since the development of the first colonial cities there has been an intense intellectual debate between those who believe in urban progress and those who believe that the nation is doomed if it allows an urban civilization to develop. The argument is frequently fuzzy. People who live their whole lives in cities speak eloquently of life in the country, and Jimmy Carter was certainly not the first president to capitalize on his small-town background.

Abraham Lincoln moved from the wilderness to the small town of Salem, Illinois, to the larger village of

Springfield, and before becoming president he practiced corporate law in Chicago. Yet when he ran for president, he buried his urbanity and his worldly ambition and adopted the guise of humble log-splitter, an image he had been working all his life to remove. Sixty years later Warren Harding could not wait to shed small-town Ohio for big-city politics, but as president he frequently praised life in the country. A popular song of World War I asked, "How you gonna keep 'em down on the farm after they've seen Paree?" Implicit in this question are both the attractive lure of the city and the solidity of rural life.

Early American Views of the City:
Hamilton and Jefferson
Many, if not most, of America's greatest writers and thinkers of the nineteenth century were anti-urban, even though a good number of them, including Edgar Allan Poe and Walt Whitman, lived in the cities they professed to hate. The intellectual historians Lucia and Morton White have written about the animosity toward the city that has pervaded American thought. The Whites found that a lot of people who believed in the basic American values they had learned in farming communities feared the new city and its technology. The unchallenged father of this philosophy of urbanism is Thomas Jefferson.

Jefferson was a Virginia planter, an inventor, a lover of all things French, and a dedicated anti-urbanite. He firmly believed that the future goodness of America rested in the hands of that rural group whom he called the "yeoman farmers." His chief political enemy was Alexander Hamilton of New York, an urbane, sophisticated man who believed that the nation's greatness rested on the rapid growth of capitalism through the stimulation of trade and commerce in urban centers. The rival political parties that grew up around these two men formed their platforms in large measure around this urban-rural conflict. Along with Jefferson's hostility toward the city went a belief in an informed democracy, which he believed could exist only outside of cities, where people controlled their own labor.

Hamilton believed in rule by an elite. Part of his vision of cities was that they necessarily attracted a lower class of working people, "a mob," in whose hands he believed no political power should reside. In his defense of the Constitution he wrote, "All communities divide themselves into the few and the many. The first are the rich and the wellborn, the other the mass of the people. . . . The people are turbulent and changing; they seldom judge or determine right." For Hamilton the city provided the logical place in which to organize such a populace.

Hamilton liked the English way of doing things as much as Jefferson liked the ways of the French. Great Britain was moving rapidly in the direction of becoming an urban, industrial nation, and Hamilton believed that the United States should follow England's lead. His financial plans for the new nation (Hamilton served as our first Secretary of the Treasury) rested heavily on the idea that we should resume trading relations with Great Britain as quickly as possible, because he believed that the British were our natural commercial partners in a growing capitalistic system. Hamilton wanted a central bank with control of the nation's finances in the hands of merchants and bankers in commercial centers such as New York, Philadelphia, and Boston. Jefferson feared that this kind of banking would remove political control from those who should naturally have it in a democracy, his "yeoman farmers." Because of the deep divisions between these two men, their supporters formed two rival political factions. In this way urbanization contributed to the rise of the first political parties in America.

Writing in 1781 in his *Notes on Virginia,* Jefferson stated: "The mobs of great cities add just so much to support of pure governments as sores do to the strength of the human body." Sixteen years later in a letter to his colleague, Benjamin Rush, Jefferson sounded the same theme: "I view great cities as pesitilential to the morals, the health, and the liberty of man."

Jefferson's views were founded on a much more elaborate tradition than mere political opposition to Alexander Hamilton. In the Judeo-Christian literary tradition as preached in colonial pulpits, the city was equated with evil, and the Biblical cities of Sodom and Gomorrah were held before colonial congregations as the epitome of urban vice. The classical economist Adam Smith, whose ground-breaking theory of capitalism, *The Wealth of Nations,* was published in the same year that the American Revolution broke out, shared Jefferson's admiration for the farmer as being by nature purer than the city dweller. Wrote Smith, "to cultivate the ground is the natural destination of man."

For Smith and for Jefferson, people who lived in rural areas were "self-reliant," and self-reliance became a hallmark of the American credo. As Jefferson argued, those who worked in "manufactures and handicraft arts" could not be self-reliant because of their occupations. They were "dependent on casualties and caprice of customers." He went on to explain, "Dependence begets subservience and venality, suffocates the germ of virtue, and prepares fit tools for the design of ambition." By this Jefferson meant that merchants who depended on customers' changing tastes lost all sense of what was good and true.

In Jefferson's use of the word *ambition* can be found another source of the rural-urban tension. The Protestant theology of the colonial period counted ambition or pride as the first sin. Yet almost in spite of themselves the Puritans prospered as their towns and cities grew. As they watched the expansion of their economy and their cities, their ambition for their children, if not for themselves, grew with it. For unlike England, America was not a land of primogeniture where only the oldest son had any hope of inheritance. Colonial parents could dream of prosperity and material success for all of their children. This sense of unlimited material opportunity was as alive in the city as in the country, perhaps even more so.

Nineteenth-Century
Arguments about Cities
Ralph Waldo Emerson, a New Englander who generally viewed the city with distrust, expressed the confusion that many people felt when he wrote, "I wish to have rural strength and religion for my children, and I wish city facility and polish. I find with chagrin that I cannot have both." Perhaps as a student of the classics Emerson recalled Horace's confusion on the same subject. Sighed Horace, "In Rome you long for the country; in the country—oh inconstant!—you praise the distant city to the stars."

Emerson's friend and neighbor, Henry David Thoreau, felt no such confusion. Thoreau kept to the woods and was far more typical of the literary leaders of the day when he wrote bluntly, "I don't like the city better, the more I see it, but worse." Thoreau and Emerson were part of the first truly American literary generation; it was a literary generation that was largely anticity in its outlook. However, this literary group blossomed during the period 1820–1860, an era that saw the first big boom in American urbanization. Even as they wrote, the facts of immigration and industrialization overwhelmed their philosophical position. In the years before the outbreak of the Civil War the urban population of the country multiplied eleven times.

Urban growth during those years defeated forever Jefferson's plan for a rural America. However, the problems generated by that growth lent new truth to his words. The cities of the nineteenth century were places of disease and dirt that reinforced Jefferson's notion that cities were breeding grounds of pestilence or disease. Scientists had not yet discovered that germs caused disease. Many people believed that doing evil things caused people to get sick. It was easy for rural clergy to see cities as places where God rewarded the godless with disease and death. The sure rewards of vice (and the city had long been considered to be the home of vice) were death and disease. Nineteenth-century statistics tended to support this theory.

In the 1830s, for example, New Orleans was already famous for its criminals, and that city also had the highest death rate of any city in the nation. In 1832, 1849, and 1867 major epidemics of cholera broke out in all of the nation's cities. These outbreaks were easily interpreted as messages from on high, divine retribution for immoral urban life. Malaria, consumption, and yellow fever were constant companions of the urban-dwellers of the nineteenth century.

Death rates throughout the population were high but always soared highest among the poorer sections of the city, where crime and vice were also highest. Before the acceptance of modern medical theories the explanation for this correlation rested on assumptions about the nature of the "lower classes." That these unfortunate people had outdoor bathrooms that emptied directly into their streets, that they lived in houses with no ventilation, and that hogs running loose in the alleys provided the only form of garbage collection mattered little to self-righteous municipal leaders. Children in one-room schoolhouses across the nation were learning the saying of John Wesley, a famous minister, "Cleanliness is next to godliness." To be filthy was to be ungodly, and many people believed that the epidemics of the cities were nothing less than the wrath of God falling down on the heads of urban-dwellers.

The scientific discoveries of the nineteenth century brought changes in the cities that had a revolutionary impact on the way people thought about urban life. The argument between the city boosters and the city detractors was no longer as simplistic as it once had been. The establishment of municipal boards of health and departments of sanitation brought about a decline in the incidence of major epidemics without any noticeable decline in the amount of vice and crime. In fact the latter was on the rise.

Darwinism and the Spread of Cities

A new theory arose to underpin the anti-urban argument. Taking their lead from the experiments that Charles Darwin performed with plants during the middle of the nineteenth century, intellectuals argued that Darwin's theory of the "survival of the fittest" could be applied as easily to people as to plants. If one agreed with Darwin that the fittest survived, then it stood to reason that those who survived the disease and crime of mid-nineteenth-century American cities were the heartiest of human beings. By the end of the century this argument had taken on a new twist. Urban reformers, sometimes called "Reform Darwinists," believed that by changing the conditions of the cities more people would be fitter, and more people would survive. It was not that cities were believed to be any better but that people believed that the vice, the corruption, and the diseases could be eradicated.

It is not surprising that by the middle of the nineteenth century many Americans, although still distrusting the cities in theory, had come to a position where they wished to wipe out the city's ills and not the city itself. Unlike Jefferson, Thoreau, and other early writers, most nineteenth-century Americans believed in material progress. That is, they believed that the accumulation of money and wealth meant that a person or nation was moving ahead. The city was the most obvious site of this type of American growth.

Frontier areas had always scrambled to develop cities as rapidly as possible. The Treaty of Greenville of 1795, signed by the United States and England, meant that settlers in the Ohio and Mississippi valleys would be protected from Indian attacks. Settlers poured into these areas. Between 1800 and 1850 these settlers established the cities of Cincinnati, Pittsburgh, Louisville, Memphis, and St. Louis. Almost all of these cities had been military forts first. As had been true of the older colonial cities, agriculture followed the establishment of trading centers, not vice versa. Many of these midwestern cities were laid out along lines set down for urban development by none other than Thomas Jefferson himself in his provisions for town planning in the Land Ordinance of 1785.

While New England writers and thinkers were bemoaning the growth of urban areas, the citizens of these new cities were boasting of their growth in an attempt to attract more citizens to their towns. Civic boosters equated bigger with better and the city with wealth and progress. As soon as a western town established a newspaper, that newspaper was sure to predict a population boom, prosperity, and success for its locale. In the same decade that Thoreau was writing that "the pigs in the street are the most respectable part of the [urban] population," another American wrote with civic pride, "All people take pride in their great cities. In them naturally concentrate the great minds and the great wealth of the nation. There the arts that adorn life are cultivated, and from them flows out the knowledge that gives its current of thought to the national mind."

Southerners and the City
Southerners as a group remained overwhelmingly anti-urban during the nineteenth century, but even among them one found urban supporters. Many southerners in the years both before the Civil War and after spoke against the evils of northeastern cities but championed the development of southern cities as a way to free the region from its economic dependence on the North. As long as southern planters had to send their products to northern cities to be sold or made into manufactured goods, the southern economy could be controlled by the North. Only by developing their own trading and manufacturing cities could the South break free from economic dependence on the North.

One drawback to the development of southern cities was that slavery, as the historian Richard Wade has demonstrated, could not exist as well in urban areas as on plantations. Control over both slaves and free black citizens was far more difficult in the cities. In the eighteenth century white slaveowners had argued that slavery was a "necessary evil" if the plantation system was to be successful. By the nineteenth century, however, many white southerners believed that all black people were inferior to white people and needed to be controlled.

Beyond this, the ruling white southern aristocracy held as an integral part of its creed that work in the marketplace was not as socially acceptable as agricultural work. The importance of slavery and this provincial hostility toward business worked against any real urban growth in the South until after the Civil War. At that point, however, the supporters of the "New South" were as urban in their outlook as any other Americans had ever been.

Western Cities
The West was as contradictory in its attitude toward cities as were the North and the South. Westerners tended to view the cities of the East as evil but found their own cities, which were rapidly growing throughout the nineteenth century, to be "representative of all that was virtuous in the American experiment." By 1890 Chicago was the second largest city in the United States, and its promoters knew no limits in their boasts for its strengths. Yet Carl Sandburg, the poet most closely identified with that city, could write of his metropolis in 1916: "Of my city, the worst that men will say is this: / You took little children away from the sun and the dew, / And the glimmers that played in the grass under the great sky, / And the reckless rain; you put them between walls."

The Farmer versus the City
By Sandburg's era the argument between city and country had taken on a new dimension. During the 1890s a political movement among southern and west-

ern farmers, known as populism, gave rise to the strongest anti-urban feelings since Jefferson's time. A new political party, the Populist Party, was founded on the belief that the country needed to return to farm values. The Populists believed that cities were ruining the American economy. Since the country was undergoing a severe economic depression at the time, many people believed the Populists. Under the leadership of Populist presidential candidate, William Jennings Bryan, the East, particularly the urban East, was held responsible for all the ills facing the farmers. Agriculture had experienced several severe cycles of economic depression in the years since the Civil War. Where once Jefferson had worried that the city would destroy the farm, Bryan took a more positive stance in his rural attack on the city.

In his most famous oration, the "Cross of Gold" speech, Bryan proclaimed: "Burn down your cities and leave our farms, and your cities will spring up again as if by magic, but destroy our farms, and the grass will grow in the streets of every city in the country." In this speech Bryan identified the "gold interests"—his name for eastern bankers—as the enemies of the farmers, whom he managed to identify with Jesus Christ. In a famous metaphor he challenged the eastern cities: "You shall not press down upon the brow of labor this crown of thorns. You shall not crucify mankind upon a cross of gold."

Youthful and silver-tongued, Bryan, along with the Populists, represented the last serious threat to urban politicians by a national farm movement. Even during the height of Bryan's popularity, the movement that was to seal the victory of urban America was under way. In the years between 1860 and 1920, for every person who moved to the farm twenty farmers moved to the city.

As the nation became more and more urbanized, the

values of the farmer continued to be held in high esteem in some poetry and literature. However, the contemporary rural character was subjected to a new unfamiliar mockery in many circles. Words like *rube* and *hick* crept into descriptions of those who lived on farms. The apple-cheeked, suntanned, barefoot farmboy became the stereotypic village bumpkin. The city was where the action could be found, and although most people continued to give lip service to the values of rural America, the folks who lived out those values on a daily basis were losing support.

In 1897 a Department of Agriculture bulletin warned against the evil effects of literature that ridiculed the farmer:

> The most potent influence in draining the best young people from the farm is the caricature of humanity that passes for a farmer in the pages of current literature. Simpleminded, and incidentally honest, uncouth in language and coarse in manner, destitute of everything but good intentions, he is depicted more unfavorably than is positive villainy. A creature of the imagination, a composite of everything comical, is made to represent one-half of a great people. His very name is fixed, and his horse's name is Dobbin.

Bryan himself was to suffer from bucolic stereotyping and can even be said to have died because of it. Bryan was subjected to public ridicule when he defended the most extreme views of agricultural America in the Scopes trial of 1925. Under oath Bryan explained that he believed totally all the stories in the Bible. Bryan died shortly after the trial. In his history, *The Search for Order*, Robert Wiebe has characterized Bryan: "His public life was devoted to translating a complicated world . . . back into those values he never questioned."

"Those values" were those of a simpler, rural America. They were the values of a white, middle-class, Protestant agricultural society. That society was being passed by in the early twentieth century, as a multi-national, diverse, heterogeneous mix of peoples populated the nation's cities. The Scopes trial marked one of the last victorious stands of this rural world. Bryan defended the right of the state of Tennessee to prohibit the teaching of evolutionary theories of the world's creation. In this famous trial prosecuting attorney Clarence Darrow called the fundamentalist Protestant Bryan to the stand. Darrow managed to equate Bryan's religious views with backwardness and provincialism. Although the state of Tennessee technically won the trial, the verdict was one of the last decisions for rural America over urban America. By the decade of the 1920s, for the first time more Americans lived in urban areas than on farms.

The City versus the Farm:
A Continuing Theme
Thus, it would seem that the argument between Jefferson and Hamilton was settled in the early years of the twentieth century. Yet in American thought and attitudes the conflict persisted, with the anti-urban forces holding sway most powerfully among writers and artists. As Lucia and Morton White have pointed out, anti-urbanism continued as a strong theme in American thought. Some of the finest American paintings of the twentieth century are starkly realistic portraits of the urban scene. They include works by John Sloan and William Glackens of the "Ashcan School," the very name of the style indicative of a certain disdain for their city

subjects. Another famous American painter of the twentieth century, Edward Hopper, joined their ranks with his portrayals of everyday city scenes.

Nor are painters the only ones to carry on the anti-urban theme. Writers from Theodore Dreiser and Stephen Crane at the beginning of the century to Willa Cather and Hart Crane and, more recently, Claude Brown and Ntozake Shange, have focused on the evils inherent in an urban society. In 1983 the sculptor George Rickey insisted that artists must "serve time" in a city. By the use of this phrase Rickey showed that he shared the traditional intellectual distaste for the city. In fact, he viewed it as a prison. On the one hand, cities are our cultural capitals, dictating to rural areas and small towns the current taste in art and fashion. On the other hand, the anonymity and impersonal quality of life in a large city can crush an artist's creativity. In an article in *American Artist* written in 1983, Stephen Doherty wrote, "the contrast between opportunity and deprivation in densely populated, energetic metropolitan communities has always existed . . . while cities have offered the worst of their times, they have also offered the best."

The conflict between urban and rural values has been part of the American scene since the process of urbanization began on this continent in the seventeenth century. Although those who live in cities today far outnumber those who live in rural areas, the persistence of an anti-urban intellectual tradition is strong enough that candidates for political office, even in the 1980s, must give voice to the belief that all that is good and true and American lies outside the metropolis.

3 | Cities on the Frontier

In writing about urbanization in America it is impossible not to focus on the great urban centers of the Northeast. However, from the beginning of this country cities were part of the frontier experience. Urbanization was not a localized force, a fact that should not be underestimated. Northeastern cities grew faster and bigger, but cities on the edge of each new line of frontier learned to emulate their growth and contributed their own chapter to the story of the nation's urbanization. Frontier cities often faced the same problems that bothered the older cities of the Northeast. Most important, cities on the edge of the frontier stimulated the urbanization of the country.

Urbanization Moves Westward
As soon as the American Revolution was over, the citizens of the new nation began to push west. More than one historian has shown that the westward movement was made possible by the push to establish towns, the desire to set up trading centers at the edge of the civilized areas so that the raw materials of the continental interior could be brought back to the coast. Towns and then cities sprang up in the Ohio and Mississippi river valleys and along the shores of the Great Lakes. In 1826, when the capital in Washington, D.C., was still a young city numbering only ten thousand, and herring could be netted along the shores of the Potomac, settlers had already established the river city of Cincinnati, a city of twenty-five thousand. The lake cities of Buffalo, Cleveland, Detroit, Chicago, and Milwaukee were estab-

lished and growing. Over the course of the next forty years their population would increase sixteen-fold.

These cities were raw and, to some, undesirable places. However unformed, these new cities quickly aped the improvements of the cities back East. As soon as possible, schools and churches, banks and drygoods stores were built. The wealthiest citizens also contributed opera houses and municipal theaters. The sheriff was replaced by a town police force, and private wells and springs gave way to formal municipal systems for water and sewage. More population meant progress, and urban promoters were hired to exhort settlers to choose one western town over another. Richard Wade has called the town promoter of the early eighteenth century "the true frontiersman in the development of the country."

Not all of this happened by 1830, of course, but by 1830 the pattern of frontier urbanization was well enough set that it was clear that the changes in city development that were occurring in the East—the systemization of water supplies, the regimentation of fire and police forces, and the development of municipal services for the poor and disabled—were bound to occur almost simultaneously in the urban areas spread across the continent.

One easy way to envision the urbanization of the frontier is to look at the westward movement of the nation's center as measured in terms of population. Twenty-five years after the Revolution the center of population was located near Baltimore. By the time of the Civil War it was located in Ohio, and by 1920 the center of the United States was located in Indiana.

Yet another way to view the important connection between the American frontier and urbanization is to recall that even the eastern cities were once frontier settlements. To the earliest English settlers, New York, Boston, Philadelphia, and Richmond were at first frontier outposts of the most desolate nature. As each succeeding generation of settlers explored a new frontier, so too did each succeeding generation develop its own cities on those frontiers.

The "River Cities"

The second great wave of cities was developed in the Mississippi and Ohio river valleys. Collectively called the "river cities" by most urban historians, Cincinnati, Pittsburgh, Louisville, Memphis, St. Louis, and New Orleans shared a common heritage, and they hold a common place of importance in the history of urbanization. As Paul Kramer has written in *The City in American Life*, "What happened [to them] became part of the total fabric of urban America and served as a guide and inspiration for the railroad cities and the big cities that were yet to come." To begin with, many of these cities had been the location of early military forts. Pittsburgh was first Fort Duquesne and then Fort Pitt, its name changes reflecting the shifting fortunes of the colonial armies that warred on the outskirts of civilization. Cincinnati had once been Fort Washington, and Louisville, New Orleans, and St. Louis were all prized originally for their strategic value.

The early settlers of these cities shared a common faith that the destiny of these areas was urban. When St. Louis was no more than a limestone hill and Missouri was not yet even a territory, a group of men surveyed the area and determined that this site "might become, hereafter, one of the finest cities in America." By 1800 one thousand people lived in St. Louis, a large number, especially when one considers that the nineteenth-century definition of *urban* mandated a population of 2,500 and the fact that much of the land between St. Louis and the Appalachians had almost no form of settlement.

The Coming of the Railroad

Another common characteristic of the frontier cities in the nineteenth century was their active involvement in the construction of the railroad. Until the coming of the railroad, travel and trade to and from the river cities was slow, and water provided the major form of transportation. Transportation had long determined the location of cities. Railroad centers would now take the place of seaports and riverbanks as locales for urban growth. Urban boosters knew this. Various small towns fought hard to have the rail lines pass through their communities.

The financial struggle in the campaign to attract railroads to various locales revealed yet another trait of the frontier city. Because of the concentration of population in these areas, the cities dominated the politics within their respective states. This factor was initially very important in getting states to appropriate the funds necessary for railroad development. In order to construct railroads, cities had to float bond issues that meant great increases in their municipal debts. In most cases permission for this kind of financing came from state legislatures. In the democratic system within which most states operated, population determined numbers of legislators. In this way the more populous cities could count on their numbers in state legislatures to help them win the votes necessary for the approval of railroad funding. As the tracks were laid, more people migrated to the cities located near the railroad. The cycle continued; with more people the city had more political power within the state.

This pattern has remained true of many urban areas throughout the United States. State and national political candidates, for instance, often campaign only in urban areas. Capturing the majority of the votes in these areas is far more important than winning all of the votes in outlying small towns and villages. In an area of concentrated population it is easier to reach large numbers of people all at once. This dominance of the city in state politics was first apparent as frontier cities moved territories toward statehood.

Another, opposite political problem arose at the same time. Some rural leaders, realizing the power that they would lose to the growing urban centers, arranged the geographical limits of political areas so that areas of smaller population could keep control over state politics. This pattern of the overrepresentation of sparsely populated agricultural areas has remained a factor in local politics in many states.

Frontier Cities as Cultural Centers

Not only were cities on the frontier sources of political power, the frontier city also represented the cultural center for the surrounding territory. In the area of the first frontier, the old Northwest Territory (now the states of Michigan, Ohio, Illinois, Indiana, and Wisconsin), federal legislation in the form of the Northwest Ordinance had ordained the establishment of public schools in every town. As towns grew to be cities, education flourished. The frontier city took very seriously its responsibility for educating the local populace. In Cincinnati, for example, by 1850 there were, in addition to the public elementary and secondary schools, three liberal arts colleges, nine specialized colleges, four medical schools, one law school, and a host of private academies. The frontier city, the center of culture and education, in this way played a social role that would be typical of any area undergoing urbanization in the nineteenth century.

Land Speculation and the Frontier City
Modern cities have deep roots in the development of the frontier city. One such legacy is a belief in material progress. Often on the frontier this progress was sought and found in land speculation. Booms in real estate prices attracted settlers to a location. Once the population was there, the city grew, feeding on itself as its citizens demanded and provided a variety of goods and services. Land speculation was a risky business, particularly in the early nineteenth century before the regulation of the banking system.

A Virginian viewing the land speculation practices of Chicago in the 1840s created the following scene to describe the process:

A. sells a lot to B. for 10,000 dollars, B. sells to C. for 20,000 dollars, no money passing, C. writes to his friend D. in New York of the rapid rise in the price. The property had gone in a very short time from 10,000 dollars to 20,000 dollars and would double within ninety days, such was the rush of capitalists to the West, and the peculiar situation of this property, adjoining the Depot (on paper), of the "North Bend and Southern Turn Great Central Railway and Trans-Continental Transportation Company." D. immediately takes the property at 25,000 dollars, and writes to his friend E. in Boston concerning that wonderful Western place Chicago, relating how property has risen in value and regretting

that he is not able to hold on to a very desirable
and highly valuable piece of real estate he owns
in that city worth 50,000 dollars, but for which
he is willing to take 40,000 dollars.

Although this account is silly, the basic message is clear.
Capitalism flourished in frontier cities, where real estate speculation meant fortune for some and ruin for
others. Gambling on the site of a city's next area of development began in these cities. It continues today as
people buy property adjoining urban areas in the hope
that the city will spread in their direction.

As the scenario above implies, real estate speculation was closely tied to railroad development. Many
frontier towns blossomed into cities overnight as their
citizens won the battle to have the rail route pass
through their town. Other towns disappeared alto-
gether when the railroad passed them by. Billings and
Coulson, Montana, are towns that typify these two
patterns. Coulson was settled first, in 1876, and by 1882
the town had its own newspaper, whose editor, a typical frontier promoter, predicted that Coulson would
become a great urban center whose economic base
would rest on shipments of Montana cattle by rail back
East. Coulson had by that time, in addition to the
newspaper, a hotel, five saloons, three general stores,
and a brewery. However, when the Northern Pacific
Railroad laid its track through Montana, Coulson was
passed by. A group of land speculators, including one
Frederick Billings, a former president of the railroad
company, had purchased a plot of land west of Coulson. Through a series of financial deals with the Northern Pacific and political deals with the Montana legis-
lature, the speculators ensured that the railroad track

The frontier was speckled with cities like Dodge City, Kansas (shown here in 1878), whose fates were closely tied to the route of the railroad.

would pass through their newly created town, Billings, Montana. They got rich, Billings grew rapidly as a railroad city, and Coulson, Montana, became a ghost town.

Billings's growth was not only rapid but typical of the growth of the frontier city. Real estate prices quadrupled, but in spite of the new high prices housing soared. In the first few months after the railroad track reached the town, construction was reported as follows: "April 26, two houses; May 26, fifty-one houses; June 26, eighty-one houses; July 26, 124 houses; and on October 26, 7,250 houses." Billings was well on its way to becoming a city. Over the course of the next decade the urbanization of this town would bring with it problems of municipal organization, water supply, sewage disposal, education, and fire protection, among others. The assumption of greater municipal government responsibility for community concerns followed the pattern of urbanization in the older cities of the East.

Morality and the Frontier City
Back East, however, as we have read, the city was considered to be the center of vice and corruption. By contrast, westerners often found their cities to be agents of morality and civilization. The reason for this was simple. On the frontier women were scarce in the early days of many pioneering movements. As settlements stabilized, however, and families arrived, the presence of women was believed to be a good moral influence. In nineteenth-century America women were widely supposed to be the upholders of moral virtue, and for many westerners the frontier city, under the influence of its female citizens, was considered to be a more righteous place than the rough-and-ready male world of the mining camp or the ranch. In 1867 a citizen of Denver, William Dixon, described the changes in that mining city

when women arrived: "As you wander about the hot and dirty streets, you seem to be walking in a city of demons. . . . A lady is a power in this country. From the day when a silk dress and a lace shawl were seen in Main Street, that thoroughfare became passably clean and quiet; oaths were less frequently heard; knives were less frequently drawn; pistols were less frequently fired."

Not everyone, however, was convinced that transplanted eastern women could cultivate the finer life in the frontier cities. There were observers who believed that western cities, like the ones back East and in Europe, were evil places bound to destroy the forces of good. Women as well as men, this argument ran, were likely to be corrupted by the city, wherever it was located. A Mrs. Josiah Royce believed this to be particularly true of the city of San Francisco during the Gold Rush days of the 1850s. In her memoirs of that time she wrote, "And then it came to pass, that in this our early California life, while we had the pleasure of associating with those who were true to their convictions, earnest in their religious life, and faithful and lovely in the domestic circle, yet, on the other hand, we often met people, who had let loose the reins of moral government over themselves and families; and consented that others should do so."

The Frontier City and Immigration
California's cities may or may not have replicated the ills of eastern urbanization as Mrs. Royce believed. Certainly they were the only frontier cities to attract a sizable population of immigrants. Unlike the cities of the East Coast, however, western cities attracted their greatest number of immigrants from Asia, not from Europe. We will discuss later the general problems fac-

ing all immigrants in American cities. However, immigrants to West Coast cities faced violent harassment that was particularly characteristic of the frontier.

Chinese immigrants began pouring into California at the time of the 1849 Gold Rush, but the influx of Asian immigrants peaked in 1882. Like their European counterparts on the other side of the continent, these Asian immigrants clustered together in cities. Frontier cities such as Seattle and San Francisco were soon known for their Asian districts, invariably called "Chinatown." On a trip to San Francisco near the end of the nineteenth century, the British novelist Rudyard Kipling toured that city's Chinese district. He described the housing as follows: "I explored a house about four stories high . . . and began to burrow down, having heard that these tenements were constructed on the lines of icebergs—two-thirds below sight level. . . . Great is the wisdom of the Chinaman."

Kipling knew of the hostility directed against the Chinese. In these frontier cities they were subjected to overt discrimination in employment and to physical violence. Frontier cities were often characterized by lawlessness and a vigilante mentality that believed that citizens could take the law into their own hands. In Los Angeles and San Francisco the Chinese immigrants frequently bore the brunt of this violence. By 1890 half of the 110,000 Chinese living in America resided in frontier cities on the West Coast. Some of the nation's earliest race riots occurred in these cities; the Chinese were the target. In 1871 several Chinese were killed in a riot in Los Angeles, and in 1877 San Francisco rioters destroyed thousands of dollars worth of Chinese homes and businesses in that city. In an area so newly brought to civilization the tendency to pick up weapons to settle quarrels was all too common. The citizens of the frontier city resorted too frequently to their own brands of "justice."

In 1882 the frontier city received federal aid in solving the "problem" of the Chinese. That year Congress passed a law restricting the numbers of Asians who could migrate to the United States. As we will learn in the next chapter, the population of eastern cities was just beginning to explode with immigration in the decade that the California frontier demanded limits to its foreign-born population. Cities on the frontier were almost always more homogeneous than those on the East Coast, and they seemed determined to remain so. As a matter of fact, the cities of the Mississippi and Ohio valleys, the Great Plains, and the West Coast were often heterogeneous only with respect to religion, and even there the divisions were most likely to be created among squabbling Protestant sects.

Overview: The Frontier City
The frontier is most often associated in our minds with wilderness and Indians, with cowboys and ranchers, mining and outlaws. Hollywood movies and television have reinforced the image of the lone pioneer striking out away from civilization. Yet most of the settlers who left the East to travel to the Midwest, the Great Plains, or California planned to build cities on the frontier. Dodge City and Carson City were not named accidentally. The entrepreneurs who moved west, whether to mine or farm or ranch, planned to prosper, and in the American vision prosperity meant urbanization. Although the cities in the interior and along the West Coast did not grow as rapidly as those in the Northeast, at least during the nineteenth century, they were still important in the nation's urbanization process. These cit-

ies established patterns of government and economic development and wrestled with the problems of immigration and rapid expansion. As urban historians have pointed out, urbanization in the United States coincided with the opening of the frontier. Unlike the cities of Europe, the cities of the American frontier were not dependent on a previously established agricultural economy. They were places of risk and venture that often sprang up overnight on a prairie with little but the hope of a coming railroad track to inspire their settlement.

4

Immigration and the City:
1820–1910

During the nineteenth century there were two great surges of growth in American cities. The first occurred during the four decades preceding the Civil War, and the second occurred between the end of the Civil War and the outbreak of World War I. Both were fueled by the same force—immigration, the flocking of thousands of Irish, mainland Europeans, and Asians to American cities.

Early Population Growth
At the time of the American Revolution the United States was overwhelmingly rural. Philadelphia, along with the next four largest cities—New York, Boston, Charleston, and Newport—comprised less than 4 percent of the total population of the thirteen colonies.

The total population of the country almost doubled in the first quarter-century after independence, but the nation remained overwhelmingly rural. By the census of 1790 there were still only twenty-four cities with a population over 2,500. By 1820 this picture of population distribution had not changed much. Two-thirds of the urban population lived in the twelve cities which in that year had a population of more than ten thousand. The increase in population between 1790 and 1820 had little to do with immigration as the United States would come to know it. Although it is true that all but the native American Indians were immigrants, neither the Americans of the time nor historians later have considered the steady emigration from Great Britain, Scotland, and Germany in these early years to be immigration in the sense that the later waves of foreign-born to the cities would be. The census of 1790 showed that 10 percent of the population was Scotch-Irish in origin and another 9 percent was German. Imported African slaves accounted for another large percentage of the immigrants, although it is important to realize that this group immigrated to the new nation against its will.

Immigration: 1820–1860
What the German, the Scotch-Irish, and the African immigrants of the late eighteenth century had in common was their tendency to reside in rural areas. Although their influence would be felt in many ways throughout the course of American history, they had no single, concentrated impact because they were spread out over the agricultural areas of the nation. Between 1820 and 1860 more than 5 million Europeans arrived on American shores, attracted by the promise of jobs and anxious to flee the revolutions and famine of the Old World. One-third of this group hailed from Ireland and 20 percent came from Germany. Many, if not most, of these people had lived in rural areas of Europe and Ireland, but they landed in cities and, poverty-stricken, stayed in the urban areas where their boats first docked. A typical Irish immigrant of the 1840s was a poor farmer named Patrick Kennedy who had enough money to get to Boston and no farther. His son would become mayor of Boston and his great-grandson, John F. Kennedy, would become president of the United States in 1960.

The coming of these vast numbers of immigrants stimulated the development of the northeastern United States as the nation's urban center. At a time when well over three-quarters of the nation's people still lived in small towns and on farms, states like Massachusetts, Rhode Island, Ohio, and Pennsylvania were increasingly urban in character. And this urbanization was di-

rectly connected to immigration. Although the proportion of foreign-born Americans in the country as a whole
never rose above 15 percent before the Civil War, by
the 1850s over half of the residents of Boston and New
York had been born outside the United States.

After the Civil War:
The New Immigration
The flow of immigrants to the United States between
1820 and 1860 was just the beginning. In the fifty years
after 1860 the population of the nation as a whole
jumped from 31,443,321 to 91,972,266, and the urban
population increased from 6,216,518 to 44,639,989. In
1860 fewer than 20 percent of all Americans lived in cities, but by 1910 almost half of the population (45.7 percent) lived in cities. During these fifty years immigration was a leading factor in the growth of urban areas.
By 1890 New York City would be able to boast that it
contained twice as many German-born people as the city
of Hamburg, twice the Irish of Dublin, and half as many
Italians as the city of Naples. In fact, the census of 1890
revealed that 80 percent of all residents of New York
City were born to foreign parents or had themselves
been born outside the United States.

Unbelievably, the enormous waves of immigrants
in the last two decades of the nineteenth century marked
the beginning, not the end, of the greatest influx of immigrants to the United States. More than 14 million more
immigrants arrived in America between the turn of the
century and the end of World War I. Nearly all of them
resided in northern cities because that was where they
found their greatest opportunities for employment. By
1900 more than two-thirds of the foreign-born lived in
cities, and the figure would climb much higher after
World War I.

Many of the immigrants pouring into America during the late nineteenth and early twentieth centuries concentrated in the cities of the Northeast. This photo shows Mulberry Street on New York's Lower East Side in the early 1900s.

The immigrants who arrived at the end of the nine-teenth century and the beginning of the twentieth cen-tury were different from those who had arrived earlier. They did not come from the British Isles and Germany. They came instead from southern and eastern Euro-pean countries. Their complexions were dark, they did not speak English in their native countries, and they were far more likely to be Roman Catholic or Jewish than they were to be Protestant. Their diversity changed the cities where they lived. In *The Magnificent Ambersons* Booth Tarkington described the reaction of an Anglo-Saxon, Protestant American walking through his city during a period of great immigration:

> George walked through the begrimed crowds of hurrying strangers and saw no face that he re-membered. Great numbers of the faces were even of a kind he did not remember ever to have seen; they were partly like the old type that his boyhood knew, and partly like types he knew abroad. He saw German eyes with American wrinkles at their corners; he saw Irish eyes and Neapolitan eyes, Roman eyes, Tuscan eyes, eyes of Lombardy, of Savoy, Hungarian eyes, Balkan eyes, Scandinavian eyes—all with an American look to them. He saw Jews who had been Ger-man Jews, Jews who had been Russian Jews, Jews who had been Polish Jews, but were no longer German or Russian or Polish Jews.

The presence of thousands of diverse immigrants in post–Civil War urban areas made American cities more exciting, richer places—and also made them more problematical for the cities' leaders. As Robert Weibe has observed, the "strangeness" of the city's population during these years contributed to rural America's belief that the city "was fundamentally different and thoroughly dangerous." The "Americans" who had lived in the cities for several generations came to realize that the city could no longer be organized along the lines of community cooperation that still marked life in the smaller towns and villages. As Weibe puts it, "The city dweller could never protect his home from fire or rid his streets of garbage by the spontaneous voluntarism that had raised cabins along the frontier." The pressure of immigration meant change for municipal governments and institutions.

Immigration and Municipal Problems:
Crime and Poverty

Much of this change resulted from urban reactions to the problems caused by the new urban growth. These problems would become constants in the American urbanization process. Crime and poverty were the most serious and immediate of these problems. Crime and poverty had long been linked in the large urban areas of the Old World, and in this respect the seaboard cities of the United States proved no exception. Immigrants, because of their living conditions, were immediately tied to the rising rate of both poverty and crime.

By 1852 it was estimated that half of the people on public assistance in the eastern seaboard cities were German and Irish, and in New York City in 1860, 86 percent of those officially categorized as "paupers" were foreign-born. By 1900 poverty among the immigrant sections of major cities was epidemic. In that year newspaper reporter Jacob Riis described in somber detail the connection between poverty and crime in the life of one young immigrant boy: "Jacob Beresheim was fifteen when he was charged with murder. . . . He was born in a tenement . . . where the Tenement House Committee found 324,000 persons living out of sight and reach of a green spot of any kind, and where sometimes the buildings, front, middle, and rear, took up ninety-three percent of all the space on the block. . . . The sunlight . . . never entered there. Darkness and discouragement did and dirt. . . . the tenement taught him gambling as its first lesson, and stealing as the next."

Although other stories of poverty and crime might not have been as dramatic as this one told by Riis, it was clear that the rising number of paupers in crowded urban areas led to a rising crime rate. Throughout the seventeenth and eighteenth centuries there had been crime, of course, but it had followed predictable patterns. Robbery had accounted for much of this early crime, and the wealthy had taken it on themselves to provide private security for their homes and warehouses. After 1830 the spread of crime of all kinds meant that a few rich merchants could no longer be responsible for the protection of an entire city, especially when the criminals were as likely to perpetrate crimes against those in the poorer sections of the city as they were against the wealthier classes.

Responses to Urban Problems:
Police and Fire Departments
In this way immigration and the rapidly rising population stimulated the organization of a more formal police force. As was the case with so many American institutions, the United States took its lead in police protection from the British. This had been true from the earliest volunteer citizen patrols. The "Watch and Ward" system of neighborhood protection widely used in

eighteenth-century American cities was a British organization. A night watchman, paid for by the wealthy inhabitants of a neighborhood, walked the streets looking for sources of fire and crime. As these volunteer systems proved inadequate in the mushrooming nineteenth-century cities, many municipalities patterned their police organizations on Britain's Scotland Yard. Scotland Yard, for example, had pioneered in issuing uniforms to police. By 1844 New York had policemen on the municipal payroll, and by 1853 the city furnished these police with uniforms. In this way the New York police became recognizable as the first of many branches of the modern municipal government. Philadelphia followed suit with the establishment of a police force in 1850, Boston in 1854, and Baltimore in 1857.

These early police departments, however, were often controlled by politicians. Because the pay scale for the policemen was so low, the temptation toward corruption was great. A policeman who wanted a good life for his family could be easily tempted to take money from a saloonkeeper and then look the other way when the saloonkeeper broke the liquor or gambling regulations. The combination of political and police graft kept municipal law enforcement agencies from truly serving the people until the reform movements at the end of the nineteenth century. Another result of the low pay scale was the increasing tendency of northeastern urban police forces to be staffed by Irishmen. The Irish, the earliest of the nineteenth century's waves of new immigrants, were discriminated against in employment and were forced into menial jobs by unfair hiring practices. They quickly filled police posts that were scorned by citizens who had lived in the United States longer than the Irish had. In this way the effect of immigration on urbanization had come full circle. The immigrants, by their numbers in crowded areas, had created a need that some among them came to fill.

Just as the establishment of the police force was necessitated by the increasing population brought about by immigration, so too did other municipal services spring into being during the nineteenth century. Fire departments followed much the same pattern as that of the police. New York's first fire prevention system, inaugurated in Dutch New Amsterdam, consisted of a few hundred fire buckets issued to homeowners, who were supposed to turn out in aid of one another when the fire bell sounded. Benjamin Franklin was once a volunteer fireman in the city of Philadelphia, a job that reflected his high status in that community. For the first two centuries of life in the New World it was the responsibility of the wealthier citizens, whether in colonial Philadelphia, Boston, or New York, to arrange for the fighting of fires. Along with their rank in society, they believed, went a certain duty to serve the common needs of that society. This idea of civic noblesse oblige—that those who were rich had a duty and responsibility toward society as a whole—came straight from England, where the leading citizens served in municipal positions without pay, accepting the responsibility of city government as the burden of their position in society.

However, as the immigrants swelled the nineteenth-century cities, city officials realized that a hand-

Firefighters work to contain the 1911 Triangle Shirtwaist factory fire in New York.

ful of volunteers could not cope with the fires that broke out, particularly in the poorer districts. Fire fighting, along with police protection, became a municipal task paid for by city taxes. The famous Chicago fire of 1871 helped spur the movement toward systematic fire fighting. The perhaps mythical O'Leary barn, which was reported to be the setting for the fire, was located in an immigrant area. When the three-day blaze had ended, the Chicago fire had claimed eighteen thousand dwellings, many of them poorly constructed wooden tenements that had been built to house the city's expanding immigrant population.

All of the major conflagrations of the late nineteenth and early twentieth centuries occurred in cities—the Boston fire of 1872, the San Francisco fire of 1906, and New York's Triangle Shirtwaist Factory fire of 1911. In all of these cases the extent of the fire was connected to the poor conditions caused by the sprawling growth of the cities that had come with immigration. Once again the force of immigration had been instrumental in the advancement of urbanization. In the case of fire prevention the process involved the development of new municipal controls over more than the fire departments. Contractors and builders now had to comply with municipal codes. By the 1890s most cities had specialized building codes, fire codes, and as early as 1892, electrical codes. Although abuses of the system would always exist, city governments were realizing the need for control over the ways in which the city expanded and the ways in which cities sheltered their citizens.

Education, Immigration, and the City
Sanitation, schooling, poorhouses, and orphanages were all likewise absorbed under the growing umbrella of city

government. This bureaucratic growth—the mush-rooming of city agencies—was the response of the city to problems that had always existed but were aggravated by the large number of immigrants. Of these, education was perhaps the most positive and long-lasting. The immigrants in American cities wanted nothing so much as they wanted education for their children. To many, freedom meant the freedom to learn. They came to the United States believing that the streets were paved with gold. The harsh reality of life in the city disabused them of this belief very quickly, but another of the fabled tales of America proved to be true. In these cities every child could have a free public education.

As highly glorified as the rural one-room schoolhouse has been in American folklore, it was the city, with its public libraries, museums, art galleries, symphonies, schools and universities, that provided the richest educational opportunities. Kindergartens, night schools, and vocational schools were innovations of an urban system of education stretched to accommodate the various needs of a diverse population. In a review of education in the *Atlantic Monthly* in the spring of 1899 the author, C. M. Robinson, described the impact of immigrants on lecture series sponsored by city universities. These lectures were given at night for immigrants yearning for education. Robinson wrote, "The success of the Urban Extension lectures, and the wide adoption of the system, make it a feature of urban life. . . . Within the last few months, a number of lectures on sanitation, civil government and American History have been given in Italian and colloquial Hebrew."

This same writer described other urban features that opened up to the immigrants—at no cost—educational opportunities that had been unknown to them in European countries, where learning, music, art, and books were the privileges of the wealthy. Wrote Robinson proudly, "Our public libraries are said to-day [*sic*] to contain more books than those of France, Great Britain and Germany combined. . . . Boston's splendid building and magnificent administration give evidence of municipal largess and breadth of view. In Chicago the three great libraries . . . show how generously individuals add to official provision. The public library of New York . . . illustrates a city's combination and use of private beneficence."

In the case of libraries, art galleries, symphonies, and opera houses, the city governments combined with private charity to provide a richer life for all classes in the New World. Much of this cooperation was stimulated by a concern for the future of democracy. Farsighted leaders dreamed of creating a skilled, educated urban populace from the masses of poor immigrants crowding the city streets.

Immigration and Anti-urban Sentiment
Thus, the vision of many third- and fourth-generation white Protestant urbanites was to make the city a better place by meeting the needs of the new population. There were many others, however, who wished to curtail immigration and limit the size and diversity of the cities. Increasing racism and religious prejudice arose among white Protestant Americans during the nineteenth century and was a negative result of the confluence of the two forces of immigration and urbanization.

In this way immigration was tied to the uneasiness about urban growth that was described earlier. In the 1800s anti-urban feeling was often synonymous with anti-ethnic feeling. Writing in his best-seller, *Our Country*, in 1885, the Protestant minister Josiah Strong maintained that the city was a "serious menace to our civilization." By *city* he meant that socialism and Roman Catholicism, both associated with immigration in the nineteenth-century American mind, were threatening the Protestant, capitalist order of things. At the end of the century Strong was still railing against "the foreign element." In a book titled *The Twentieth Century City* Strong warned, "We cannot shut our eyes to the fact that the foreign population, as a whole, is depressing our average intelligence and morality in the direction of the dead-line of ignorance and vice."

Strong was not alone in his fear and loathing of immigrants and their effect on the city. Robert Hunter, an early twentieth-century observer of urban conditions, wrote of immigration and urbanization in the same vein: "In certain large cities of this country almost everything separates the classes and the masses except the feeling which inheres in the word 'humanity.' The rich and well-to-do are mostly Americans; the poor are mostly foreign, drawn from among the miserable of every nation. . . . in the large cities of America, there are many things which separate the rich and the poor. Language, institutions, custom, and even religion separate the native and the foreigner. It is this separation which makes the problem of poverty in America more difficult of solution."

American Cities as "Melting Pots"
Hunter's pessimism about the future of cities containing large foreign populations and Strong's religious and ethnic prejudices are examples of one kind of thinking about immigration and urbanization in the nineteenth century. At the same time, however, it was fast becoming a cliché to call the United States a "melting pot," and it was in her cities that this "melting pot" seemed

most readily apparent. By "melting pot" people meant that the United States was similar to a huge cauldron that took in people of all nationalities and melted them together to produce a new nationality, the American. The term may have been used first by an immigrant playwright, Israel Zangwill, who wrote of America as a "seething crucible, God's crucible." Whatever divine forces were at work in melting the immigrant into an "American," the catalyst for that force was undoubtedly the city. Irish, Germans, Bohemians, Italians, Scandinavians, Russians, and many more worked and lived side by side in American cities, and their children shed Old World ways, borrowed from the traditions of each other, and called themselves Americans.

This belief that Americans were a special breed developed from a mixing of Europeans was older than the nineteenth-century immigration movement. In the 1790s Hector St. John de Crèvecoeur, a Frenchman visiting America, had asked, "What is an American?" His answer, contained in a now famous essay, foreshadowed the melting pot concept: "He is an American, who, leaving behind him all his ancient prejudices and manners, receives new ones from the new mode of life he has embraced, the new government he obeys, and the new rank he holds. . . . Here individuals of all nations are melted into a new race of men, whose labors and posterity will one day cause great changes in the world."

Although Crèvecoeur's words indicate that the melting pot theory has been around for a long time, there have been observers in every era who have argued that no true mixing of nationalities ever took place in American cities. In looking at urban America in the twentieth century, Nathan Glazer and Daniel Moynihan concluded in *Beyond the Melting Pot* that the melting pot was an image without reality. They argued that the individual nationalities and religious groups that populated the great cities rarely merged together. Furthermore, they held this separation responsible for the urban problems of the second half of the twentieth century. They saw a close connection between urbanization and immigration but felt that the two forces were far from harmonious. True as their findings may be, to the nineteenth-century observer of American urbanization, the city seemed to be a melting pot or at least a patchwork quilt of a hundred nationalities.

As immigrants poured into New York harbor in the late nineteenth century, they were unlikely to be concerned with sociological questions about how they would become Americans. The Statue of Liberty filled them with hope, and the words on its base promised them a place in a new nation. Emma Lazarus' poem issued a call to the immigrants to come to an America that would care for them: "Give me your tired, your poor,/Your huddled masses yearning to breathe free,/The wretched refuse of your teeming shore/Send these, the homeless, tempest-tost to me,/I lift my lamp beside the golden door!"

Most immigrants came to America believing in the imagery of this poem. They believed that in America all their dreams would come true. What they found was a nation in the throes of an urbanization the likes of which the world had never seen before. In many cases they were the cause of a problem, but by their very numbers forced solutions to the same problem. When their shanties proved to be firetraps, the city governments moved to ensure better housing among the poor. When immigrant poverty contributed to a rising crime rate, the police force was strengthened in ways that provided the immigrants with jobs and allowed them protection approaching that which was given to the older, wealthier citizens. In the interest of preserving democracy every attempt was made to teach immigrants English and to provide these former farmers with skills for survival in an urban society.

The immigrants trapped in the nineteenth-century American city made an indelible mark on the city's growth and development. The mixing of immigrants and the nineteenth-century city was an ultimately fortuitous merger, but cost untold numbers of human lives in the process. For every Andrew Carnegie who began life on the docks as a penniless immigrant and lived to become a millionaire, thousands more lived and died in grinding poverty, hardly more American when they died than when they had landed. But the city's response to the immigrants, both negative and positive, shaped the nature of nineteenth-century urbanization.

5

The Industrial Revolution and the City: 1820–1910

The Industrial Revolution—the coming of new machines and the factory method of manufacture—changed the face of the United States. The country at the beginning of the nineteenth century and the country at the end of the nineteenth century were hardly recognizable as the same place. Just as immigration was a nineteenth-century force closely intertwined with urbanization, so too was industrialization a force that was interconnected with the process of city growth. By the time of the census of 1900, 30 million of the country's 76 million people lived in cities, and fifty cities had populations exceeding one hundred thousand. American cities stood as the most tangible evidence of the power of the Industrial Revolution.

The Industrial Revolution and the Farm

If the cities were the most obvious evidence of the revolution in technology, the farms were not immune. Agriculture felt the effects of the Industrial Revolution keenly, and the resulting changes in farming are closely connected to the changes in the city. The steel plow, the mechanization of farm equipment, the invention of barbed wire, and the coming of electricity and the gas-powered engine all had a dual impact on the farm. First, these technological changes meant that a farmer could produce far more in less time than he had once been able to by hand. For example, in 1900 the amount of wheat or oats that one farmer could produce in an hour was four times what it had been in 1840. It took a farmer in 1900 less than three hours to harvest twenty bushels of wheat; this same production of wheat had taken sixty-one hours in 1830.

The second major result of the technological revolution on the farm had an even greater impact on the city. The new speed and efficiency of the farm machinery meant that there was a surplus of both farm supply and farm labor. This surplus of food and labor occurred at the same time that the Industrial Revolution in the cities was greatly increasing the need for thousands of unskilled laborers. Although immigrants filled much of this need, it is also true that thousands of people moved from American farms to the city, particularly in the second half of the nineteenth century. The increased efficiency and quality of food production meant that the farmers could supply the thousands of workers who lived in cities removed from food supplies. The changes in transportation meant that food could be moved to this ready market with greater ease.

The Revolution in Transportation
Of all the technological changes none had a greater impact on urbanization than the change in transportation. In 1820 all American cities were still walking cities. No one lived farther than walking distance from his or her place of employment. Factories were small, and the most formal kind of business organization was the partnership. As late as the 1830s the largest manufacturing firm in New York employed only two hundred people. The manufacturers of the early nineteenth-century cities were likely to be shipbuilders or owners of small businesses connected with shipbuilding, such as barrel-making. Cities remained primarily places of trade and commerce, not industry. The transportation revolution was to change all this.

In 1825 a canal was completed that connected Albany, New York, to that state's westernmost outpost, Buffalo. The Erie Canal marked the first stage of the transportation revolution. Any town that yearned for prosperity and progress—in short, any town that wanted to be a city—vied for a position along one of the many canals that were constructed between 1816 and 1840 at an estimated cost to the country of $125 million. Improvements in water transportation, especially the invention of the steamboat, spurred the canal movement.

However, even with the construction of miles of canals, water transportation was quickly outpaced by the railroad. In 1860 there were almost 31,000 miles of rail in the United States; in 1880, 94,000 miles; and in 1900, almost 200,000 miles. To be located adjacent to a rail line meant prosperity and growth for many small towns. For example, the small village of East Point, Georgia, grew in slightly over twenty years to become Atlanta, a leading city of the South, in large part because of its position at the juncture of two important rail lines. The same was true for Birmingham, Alabama, and countless cities throughout the Midwest.

Next in the transportation revolution came the horse-drawn buses of the 1820s, and then came the street railroad in the 1850s. Just as the railroad described above provided transportation from city to city, the street railroad provided transportation on a daily basis from small towns (soon to be called suburbs) to the city.

The 1850s saw the invention of inner-city street railways, which were horse-drawn until the 1870s. In the 1870s these street railways were converted to electric trolleys. In *Streetcar Suburbs* Sam Bass Warner Jr. details the changes in Boston and its surrounding suburbs of Dorchester, Roxbury, and West Roxbury as the

An electric streetcar in Cincinnati around 1890

city moved from being a walking city in 1850 to being a city served by electric trolleys in the late 1870s. Because of the revolution in transportation the character of this city, one of the oldest in America, was transformed.

In 1873 the electric cable car made its appearance in San Francisco, and in 1888, Richmond, Virginia, began construction of a closed-car system called an electric trolley. By 1890 50 other cities had electric trolley systems, and by 1895 the number had risen to 850. As space became an issue in the newly crowded cities (New York was the most densely populated city in the world by 1890), cities began to look for ways to remove transportation from street level. In 1878 New York constructed the first elevated railroad, the famous Sixth Avenue El. In 1895–1897 Boston laid its first 1½ miles of subway track, and New York completed its first subway line in 1904.

As late as 1890, though, 70 percent of the trolleys in the nation's cities were still horse-drawn and were responsible for the two leading forms of urban pollution—horse manure and noise. The horses' hooves and the metal wheels on the cobbled streets were loud. The poet Edgar Allan Poe complained in a letter he wrote in the 1840s: "The din of vehicles is even more thoroughly and more intolerably a nuisance. Are we never to have done with these unmeaning round stones?" Poe did not live long enough to see the solution to this problem, which came in 1878 when Washington, D.C., became the first city to use asphalt extensively on its roads. The new smooth roads were not only quieter, but they also made possible the use of another new invention, the bicycle, and helped stimulate experimentation with a vehicle that would change the twentieth-century city, the automobile.

Although the car was part of a later America, it is interesting to note that the gasoline engine was invented by the 1890s and that the most farsighted of the city planners were already preparing for the advent of the automobile revolution by the turn of the century. In spite of its newness the automobile had made an appearance by 1900, one that left an indelible mark on many of its early observers. As Henry Ford, the automobile pioneer, reminisced, "It was considered to be something of a nuisance for it made a racket and scared horses. Also it blocked traffic. For if I stopped my machine anywhere in town a crowd was around it before I could start up again. If I left it alone, even for a minute, some inquisitive person was always trying to run it. Finally I had to carry a chain, and chain it to a lamp post whenever I left it anywhere."

Communications and Urbanization
With the transportation revolution came a revolution in communications. In the 1840s the telegraph dramatically changed the speed with which news could be carried across one city and from city to city. The telegraph meant that news and information were no longer limited to the speed of transportation. Cities could expand beyond the distance that a person could walk or ride a horse. In the middle of the nineteenth century cities were crisscrossed with telegraph wires; with the invention of Guglielmo Marconi's wireless telegraph, the communication revolution marched on. Without the need for wires, the new telegraph could send messages even where lines had not been laid.

The next invention, the telephone, was the brainchild of Alexander Graham Bell. The first message to be transmitted on the new telephone was carried from one city to another, from Baltimore to Washington, D.C.

In 1878 New Haven, Connecticut, installed the first telephone switchboard, and by 1890, eighty-six cities had telephone systems. Telephones meant that business could be conducted immediately across bigger and bigger cities. The telephone allowed factories to be built on the outskirts of existing cities and helped stimulate the geographic growth of these cities.

Typewriters, adding machines, and cash registers were all technological innovations that contributed to the communications revolution. These machines were rapidly adopted by businesses and helped small offices expand into larger ones. Payrolls, bills, and advertising mushroomed with the help of these inventions and a new work force, "white collar" workers. Where once a small business had employed one or two accountants who laboriously wrote out bills and payroll lists by hand, now large companies, using many secretaries, could generate these same things by machine. No longer was it necessary for the company's bookkeepers to have an intimate knowledge of all aspects of the business's records. Instead, many people could handle parts of this record-keeping. Skill with the new machinery was more important than a knowledge of all aspects of the industry's work. As Mark Twain wrote facetiously in an 1874 essay on the subject of the typewriter, "One may lean back in his chair and work it. It piles up an awful stack of words on one page. It don't muss things or scatter ink blots around." The white collar workers formed a growing middle class that expanded the cities' residential areas.

The introduction into cities of electricity and electrical inventions marked the end of the revolution in transportation and communication for the nineteenth century. In 1882 New York installed the first electric power plant, and between 1883 and 1913 electric power spread rapidly throughout that city. After 1878 the arc lamp was adopted by a number of cities to light their streets. Thomas Edison's incandescent lamp, which glowed more brightly and lasted longer, quickly surpassed the arc lamp in efficiency and popularity, and by the end of the nineteenth century the streets of American cities were bathed at night in electric light.

Steel and the Modern City

The adoption of the Bessemer process, a milestone in the Industrial Revolution, meant another major change for urban America. A few years prior to the Civil War, William Kelly, a Kentuckian, introduced a method for turning iron ore into steel. The Kelly system was perfected by Henry Bessemer, an Englishman. Bessemer borrowed Kelly's notion that iron could be turned into steel by forcing cold air through iron that had been heated to a liquid state. The Bessemer converter had a double effect on the city. First, it stimulated the growth of huge steel cities such as Pittsburgh and Buffalo. The chemical battle that was waged between the liquid iron and the oxygen sent flames leaping into the air over steel factories, forever marking their skylines. But the Bessemer process changed the face of all cities, not just those in which the large steel factories were located. Because of the Bessemer process, cities could build up as well as out. Steel girders were the first requirement for the skyscrapers that began to dominate city sky-

The Marshall Field building in Chicago, photographed here in the 1930s, was a forerunner of today's skyscrapers.

lines after the 1880s. Men like Louis Henri Sullivan and Henry Hobson Richardson combined the new technology with art and changed American architecture forever.

Chicago, where Richardson designed one of his most famous buildings, the Marshall Field Wholesale Store, pioneered the skyscraper. By using steel in the foundations and structure of a building it was possible to build very high skeletons that could then be encased in a variety of exterior building materials. It was no accident that Chicago led the way in skyscraper construction. The downtown business area of this city was hemmed in by the presence of Lake Michigan on the east and on the other three sides by the railway system that had been constructed. The solution seemed to be to build upward, and Chicagoans embraced the new architecture as a way to keep their city in the forefront of economic and population growth.

Lofty new buildings like Louis Sullivan's Wainwright Building in St. Louis, Missouri, set a whole new tone and style for American cities by the 1890s. Buildings continued to grow upward until the construction of the Woolworth Building in New York in 1913 raised a storm of controversy.

Fifty-five stories high, the Woolworth Building was opened amid fanfare and criticism. President Woodrow Wilson was called on to christen the opening of the building by turning on its eighty thousand electric lights by remote control from a switch in Washington, D.C. Although the crowds that gathered to witness this sight were astounded and thrilled by the building's immense height, skyscrapers were beginning to meet with disapproval in some quarters. Many people believed that the high structures were unsafe. Even more widespread was a concern that the skyscraper contributed to the crowding of too many people into too small spaces and that the towering buildings cut off light and air that were badly needed for the good health of the cities' citizens. Unsure of the skyscraper's value, New York, for example, incorporated a restriction on building height into its zoning laws in 1916.

Whether it was in the growth of skyscrapers, the development of new methods of communication, or the spread of transportation technology, the nineteenth century saw the fulfillment of industrial promise that had been a part of the nation's destiny from the beginning. Because more people still lived on farms than in cities, Jefferson seemed to have won the battle of the farm versus the city. However, Hamilton's industrial, urban vision would win out in the end.

In writing of American industrial growth in the late nineteenth century in a book called *Prisoners of Progress*, Maury Klein and Harvey Kantor have listed ten factors that they feel are key to an understanding of the American industrial experience. Such items as the emergence of a market economy, the replacement of hand tools by power-driven machinery, and the revolution in transportation are included, but perhaps the most important for an understanding of American urbanization is the tenth entry on their list: "The proportion of Americans living in cities and towns increased steadily." By the time of the Industrial Revolution, urbanization had taken on new meaning. It no longer meant simply the development of towns and cities but that living in towns and cities was becoming the dominant way of life for Americans.

Labor Changes and Urbanization
A major reason for this increase was not in itself technological in nature but was certainly central to the In-

dustrial Revolution. The nineteenth century saw the development of a new business idea, the factory system. Although the birth of this system was clearly interrelated with the inventions and technology of the era, the factory system above all meant social change, and as a social change it had its greatest impact on the city.

The factory system was the third step in the evolution of manufacturing in the United States. Until the War of 1812 most products were manufactured by craftspeople operating in local shops and marketing their products to a local populace. In the economy stimulated by the upheavals of the war many of these local industries expanded to the extent that people other than the shopowner were hired to produce the goods. However, these workers were very likely to operate out of their own homes, selling the products to the shopkeeper for distribution. This method worked well in rural areas and in small towns.

The factory system not only centralized the means of production and distribution but also contributed to urbanization. Now the products were manufactured in a central location close to sources of energy, raw materials, and markets. As Klein and Kantor have explained, by 1850 the factory system had "become the dominant form of industrial enterprise; between 1860 and 1900 it expanded so spectacularly as to dwarf everything that had gone before." One of the most important results of the widespread adoption of this system was the changing relationship between the work place and the worker. The factory was large and impersonal. The city, the home of the factory, was also increasingly large and impersonal.

By and large the jobs in the new factories called for unskilled labor. Around the industrial areas of cities stretched blocks of housing where the factory workers lived. As the factories grew larger, the distance between the individual factory worker and the factory owner widened. Although the factory came to dominate the poorer neighborhoods, it was as much an object of fear as of promise. It provided jobs but was also the scene of death and disease. It stood for opportunity but also represented poverty and class distinction. The factory was a mark of the nineteenth century's prosperity, and its chimneys belched pollution that signaled the beginning of one of the twentieth century's greatest urban problems.

A newspaper article in 1874 described the factory district of Cincinnati in an account that might have been applied to any other industrial city of the period (in spite of the author's claim to the contrary):

> Probably there is no city in America which contains a quarter so hideous as that noisome district of Cincinnati. . . . An atmosphere heavy with the odors of death and decay and animal filth and steaming nastiness of every description, hangs over it like the sickly smoke of an ancient holocaust. . . . Mammoth slaughterhouses, enormous rendering establishments, vast soap and candle factories, immense hog pens and gigantic tanneries loom up through the miasmatic atmosphere for blocks and blocks in every direction. Narrow alleys, dark and filthy, bordered by sluggish black streams of stinking filth, traverse this quarter in every direction. . . . Amid these scenes and smells lives and labors . . . a large population.

Population Shifts and
the Industrial Revolution
This large and ever-growing population in urban areas was stimulated by industrialism and marks the closest

connection between the growth of industry and the growth of the city. One did not cause the other; rather, each fed on the other. The problems attendant on this growth, especially the social problems, emerged first in the city, and it was in the city that the solutions to these problems were first explored.

We have repeated again and again that the Industrial Revolution meant population growth as people poured into cities to work in the new factories. Perhaps the relationship is best seen in a comparison of the nineteenth-century population growth in the United States with the growth of population in areas that were not experiencing the phenomenal industrial growth that America was. Between 1850 and 1920, the key years of the American Industrial Revolution, the nation's population grew by more than 350 percent. During that same period of time the population of the world as a whole increased by only 55 percent. Not only was the pattern of population changing to reflect a movement from the country to the city, but the way in which Americans earned their living also was changing to reflect the new industrialism. These occupational changes also greatly affected the pattern of urbanization.

First, of course, is the shift from work in agricultural occupations to work in industrial areas. In 1820 nearly 70 percent of the American work force was occupied in agricultural jobs. By 1920 slightly over one-quarter of the working population engaged in farm-related occupations. Two other trends in labor were of even greater importance in explaining the process of urbanization. It has been estimated that in the early nineteenth century four-fifths of all American workers were self-employed. They owned their own farms and shops, and the profits from their labor went directly into their pockets. By the early twentieth century this figure was almost completely reversed. By that time 80 percent of American laborers worked for someone else. At the same time that this pattern of industrial employment was developing, the percentage of Americans who earned a living was increasing.

What this means is that Jefferson's greatest fear had come true. The American citizen in the age of the Industrial Revolution was far from self-reliant. As the Industrial Revolution intensified, workers depended more and more on other people for jobs and salaries. The lack of independence spread to their living conditions. People in large cities were more and more dependent on a smaller and smaller number of people for their food. In overpopulated, congested urban areas people lived in smaller and smaller spaces and in much closer contact with each other. The individualistic free enterprise that is a hallmark of the American capitalist economy was leading to the growth of urban centers where communal responsibility was the only means of survival and "rugged individualism" was an anachronism.

The Changing Nature of Cities

Industrial expansion meant that growing cities followed certain patterns. Cultural and social changes happened because of changes in the economy; sometimes these changes were good and sometimes they were bad. The city attracted all kinds of people. Many were ambitious and eager to seize the opportunities that the city had to offer. Others were parasites who came to take from the city without working for what they got. Still others were trapped by the city, and because of such factors as poor health, lack of education, or just bad luck, they lived out lives of urban poverty. The growth of cities at the end of the nineteenth century meant that all of these types became more numerous.

During the infancy of the Industrial Revolution in America the type of city that flourished was a kind of city that historians have come to call the "commercial city." Daily life in the commercial city was simple. Most people walked to work. Transportation to places outside the city rested on water. There was little immigration, and the retail business was conducted through the general store. In the commercial city the class structure that existed was a descendant of older rural distinctions. Everyone knew everyone else, and people took care of their city's poor and disabled.

In these cities trade between the outlying agricultural areas and the city's inhabitants accounted for most of the business that was conducted. There was some manufacturing but very little. Specialized technology had not yet spread, and production in the commercial city was geared to the needs of the rural areas that surrounded the urban center. For example, this was the kind of city farmers traveled to to sell their produce and to buy plows and glass and other products they could not manufacture on their farms.

The commercial city was replaced in the second half of the nineteenth century by the industrial city. The industrial city centered around a certain industry or group of industries. Individual cities were chosen by industrialists because of their accessibility to markets and sources of raw materials. After a specific business located in a particular city the expansion of the business meant the expansion of the city. As factories proliferated, support industries to help in the production and distribution of the main factory's products meant increasing growth for the city. For example, an oil company might be joined by a company that manufactured pipelines used to transport that oil.

As the labor force to supply the factories grew, service industries in the city also grew, providing clothing, shelter, food, and entertainment for the labor force. The lives of the people who worked in the factories became closely tied to the success of the industry in which they worked. In good times not only did their wages improve but the industries that provided the workers with both necessities and luxuries experienced prosperity, and the overall quality of goods and services available to the populace improved. In other words, the quality of life for the worker in an industrial city was intertwined with the success of the manufacturers. In this way the workers increasingly lost control over the quality of their own lives.

In an industrial city where one product formed the basis for the city's manufacturing, even slight changes in the national consumption of the product could have a marked effect—both good and bad—on the lives of the city's inhabitants. Typical nineteenth-century cities that concentrated on a specialized kind of manufacturing were Gloversville, New York, home of the glove industry; Bridgeport, Connecticut, with its corset manufacturing; and Troy, New York, site of the collar and cuff industry. In many of the nation's industrial cities by 1900, over 50 percent of the labor force was tied, for better or for worse, to the fortunes of one industry. In Danbury, Connecticut, 70 percent of the labor force by 1900 worked to produce fur hats; in North Attleboro, Massachusetts, 70 percent worked in the jewelry industry; and in Tarentum, Pennsylvania, glass manufacture occupied 80 percent of the city's laborers.

*Urbanization and Industrialization
—a Complex Relationship*
The intertwining of urbanization and the Industrial Revolution is so tangled that it is doubtful that it can ever be unraveled. There are those who see the burgeoning population of the city as the basis for the in-

dustrial boom, whereas others see urbanization as the effect of the great surge of industrialism. The exact cause-and-effect relationship is less important than the fact that industrialism and urbanization both occurred rapidly and simultaneously in the nineteenth century. As Horace Greeley, a famous newspaper editor of the nineteenth century wrote, "We cannot all live in cities, yet nearly all seem determined to do so."

The city of the nineteenth century offered new technological wonders, job opportunities, and a whole new value system based on a seemingly limitless material prosperity. Financial panics, crowded housing, poverty, disease, and the destruction of the traditional rural value of individualism and independence attended the growth of the city in an industrial age. But the prospect of money and the excitement of the new age proved to be greater lures than the disadvantages proved to be repellents. Furthermore, as the nineteenth century drew to a close, a generation of urban reformers looked at the city with the optimistic faith that its ills could be cured.

6   *The Reaction to Urbanization: 1890–1920*

By 1890 New York had the largest population of any city in the world. If New York represented the best of all possible worlds to some of its citizens, to many more it represented hopeless days filled with poverty, crime, and disease. And what was true for New York was true for all other urban areas, albeit on a somewhat smaller scale.

San Francisco after 1880 had joined the top ten cities and was clearly the largest city west of Chicago. During the decade of the 1880s more than one hundred cities had doubled in size, among them Omaha, Nebraska; Kansas City, Missouri; Wichita, Kansas; Duluth and Minneapolis, Minnesota; Birmingham, Alabama; El Paso, Texas; Spokane, Washington; and Denver, Colorado. The squalor that the Russian immigrant found on the Lower East Side of New York City was no better nor worse than the conditions that awaited the emigrant from Shanghai in San Francisco's Chinatown. Immigration and industrialization had joined to push American urbanization as far as Western civilization had ever seen. With this progress, however, had come innumerable problems, and in the last decade of the nineteenth century reformers began first to identify those problems and then to offer solutions for them. The solutions they posed were to change the character of urbanization in the twentieth century.

Reformers Focus on the City
From the time of John Winthrop's hopes for Massachusetts Bay as the "City on a Hill" toward which all eyes in Europe would turn, each American city had be-

lieved that it would be the biggest and the best that the world had ever seen. By 1890 it was clear that American cities were, among other things, the dirtiest, the most crowded, the most disease-ridden, the most corrupt, and the noisiest that the world had ever seen. In that year Jacob Riis shocked the nation with the publication of *How the Other Half Lives*, a carefully researched exposé of the living and employment conditions of the poor in New York City. Riis, a Danish immigrant himself, was particularly interested in chronicling the horrendous conditions in which immigrants were forced to live. The work of Riis and other newspaper reporters like him stimulated the movement toward urban reform.

In the decades after the Civil War business had taken precedence over government as the appropriate career for young men of education and wealth. However, by the end of the nineteenth century a new generation of young Americans, many of them raised in an urban environment, read the reports of reformers like Riis and took on the task of reforming the cities around them. To do this they committed themselves to playing an active role in government and politics. The prototype of this kind of reforming politician was Theodore Roosevelt. Roosevelt had been born in New York City before the Civil War and had seen the city expand tremendously during his lifetime. He was born to wealth yet was imbued with a social conscience that he inherited from his father.

In Theodore Senior's world private charity could still make a difference. Young Teddy stored up memories of watching his father dress for dinner at the city home for orphan newsboys where he was a leading patron. The urban environment that Theodore Roosevelt, Jr., inhabited as a young man in the 1880s was very different from the world of his father. Private charity was no longer enough to alleviate the suffering of the city's millions. Government regulation was the only answer.

One of Theodore's friends was none other than Jacob Riis, the reporter, who took the young Roosevelt on unforgettable prowls through the city's darkest areas. What Roosevelt and Riis found, among other things, was police corruption that blocked the path of reform. At that time one of the jobs of the police was to enforce the city housing codes. Riis wrote about this problem in an article for the *Atlantic Monthly* in 1899. In the case he cited, the code to be enforced was one regulating the amount of light a tenement should have. As Riis described it, a policeman was summoned by the president of the board of health, who questioned his judgment in the case of a particularly dark apartment that the policeman had reported as light enough. In the ensuing testimony the policeman confessed that in order to see in the hallway in question he had had to light a match.

Abuses of this type by the police force were part of the reason that Theodore Roosevelt accepted the position as head of the board of police commissioners in 1895. A generation before, this job would not have been considered suitable for a man of his wealth and education, but the pressure of urbanization convinced young men and women in the 1890s that they must take an active role in the reform of the cities. The presence of people of Theodore Roosevelt's background in the reform movement marks the dominance of the city in American culture. From the turn of the century on, the character of American society was dictated by what happened in the city, not what happened on the farm. The city became the purveyor of American values. The heroes and heroines of popular American culture increasingly were city figures rather than farm figures. For the most part these new standard-bearers came from the upper classes.

The Reformers and City Government
The reformers soon found that they could not limit their attack to the urban conditions they deplored. All of city government had to be changed. When cities were small during the colonial period and right up to the time of the Industrial Revolution, they had been easily and efficiently governed. The pressures of nineteenth-century capitalism, industrialism, and immigration, however, had put pressure on the existing city government structures that those structures could not handle. For example, governments that were organized to handle a city where almost everyone knew everyone else had difficulty caring for huge new populations.

In the face of nineteenth-century urbanization in the post–Civil War years, city governments had been taken over by the phenomenon of the city boss, a politician who ran the city government, often dishonestly. The city boss is a controversial figure in American history. Boss Tweed of New York is perhaps the most famous of these men, but there were many others besides Tweed. Bosses controlled "the machine," a system of politics that enabled them, through bribery and other forms of corruption, to make a fortune at the expense of the taxpayers. One historian has estimated that between 1866 and 1871 Tweed cost the citizens of New York $100 million.

On the other hand, in an increasingly complex industrial society, the boss and his helpers did things for the average person that no one else had the time or inclination to do. This was particularly true for the immigrants. The boss arranged to meet immigrants as they landed at the city's docks, arranged housing and a job, and in return asked for the man's vote. As C. N. Glaab and A. T. Brown have pointed out in their *A History of Urban America*, the boss was there for the immigrants when the official city government was not, when there were "no public works programs, no free lunch, food stamps or social security." In the same year that he was said to be raiding the city of New York Boss Tweed gave each of the aldermen in his control one thousand dollars to spend on charity in their wards. In Kansas City "Boss" Pendergast, a midwestern version of Tweed, made it a practice to foot the bill for free Thanksgiving and Christmas dinners for the poor.

Furthermore, in the late nineteenth century, when much of the anti-urban feeling was inseparable from anti-ethnic feeling, the boss (frequently a first- or at most a second-generation immigrant) was a source of pride and hope for the immigrants who were fighting the nativist movements to restrict immigration. Nativists believed that the only true Americans were white Protestants, especially white Protestants from Northern Europe. These nativists wanted to prevent any new immigrants who were not white Protestant or northern European from entering the United States. As Oscar Handlin wrote in *The Uprooted*, "Often the feeling of group loyalty focused upon him. . . . In the columns of every newspaper his name reflected glory on the whole community and he in turn shared its sense of solidarity."

Jacob Riis and other reporters of the late nineteenth century had little time for city bosses, and in opposing them they paved the way for a brand of journalism during the early years of the twentieth century that was known as "muckraking." The muckrakers exposed corruption wherever they found it. These reporters believed the autocratic system of the city boss to be the enemy of democracy, and they worked to expose municipal corruption.

Lincoln Steffens was undoubtedly among the most influential of these Progressive era muckrakers. In *The Shame of the Cities* he called attention to the excesses of the big city bosses and demanded a total reform of municipal government. What Steffens urged was the adoption of a system of city government like the one that had been outlined in 1895 by the National Municipal League. This model charter called for a strong mayor, an independent controller, civil service for city jobs, limits to the franchise-granting powers of the city council, and home rule for cities (as opposed to state control). Other muckrakers added to this list such reforms as initiative and recall as safeguards of the people's control over government. Through recall American voters could remove from office an elected official who was corrupt. By initiative the voters could introduce legislation.

In spite of the efforts of the muckrakers, machine politics remained a force in major American cities well into the second half of the twentieth century. Its success stemmed from the fact that the boss system rested on the spoils system. This meant that once in power the boss could arrange city contracts so that he and his political friends made money.

Franchises for the new forms of city transportation were breeding grounds for corruption, and street railways were particularly good sources of this type of corruption. The first street railway franchise had been granted in New York in 1851. In Buffalo not long after, a city boss managed to win for his favorite street railway a 999-year contract; Albany's boss went him one better with a 1,000-year contract for his favored company. Corruption in railway building meant that corners were often cut on such things as safety measures. In his best-seller published in 1894, *If Christ Came to Chicago*, William Stead estimated that in 1889 there were 257 railway "murders" (deaths caused by poor regulation of the railways), 294 in 1890, 323 in 1891, 394 in 1892, and 431 in 1893. Throughout the 1890s and early 1900s the muckrakers sifted through the fine print in city contracts and budgets to expose illegal dealings between businessmen and politicians.

Housing Reform
Perhaps no form of corruption attracted as much attention and sympathy from the reformers as did the abuses of landlords. In an article published in *Forum* magazine in 1895 Jacob Riis even suggested that modern urbanization with its overcrowding of workers might destroy the concepts of home and family as they had been known in the United States for generations. In this article, titled "The Tenement: The Real Problem of Civilization," Riis quoted the New York City Tenement-House Commission's definition of the "double-decker" dwelling, a popular form of slum housing in the 1880s and 1890s. As described in the commission's report,

> The double-decker cannot be well-ventilated; it cannot be well-lighted; it is not safe in case of fire. It is built on a lot 25 feet wide by 100 feet or less in depth, with apartments for four families in each story. . . . The stairway-well in the center of the house and the necessary walls and partitions reduce the width of the middle rooms (which serve as bedrooms for at least two people each) to 9 feet each at the most, and a narrow "light and air" shaft now legally required

*The squalid hopelessness of tenement life is captured
in this photograph by reformer Jacob Riis.*

in the center of each side wall still further lessens the floor space of these middle rooms. Direct light is only possible for rooms at the front and rear. The middle rooms must borrow what light they can from dark hallways, the shallow shafts and the front and rear rooms. . . . A five story house of this character contains apartments for eighteen or twenty families, a population frequently amounting to 100 people, and sometimes increased by boarders and lodgers to 150 or more.

Tenement had originally been used as a legal term in New York to describe any dwelling that housed more than three families. By the end of the nineteenth century, as the description above implies, tenement invariably meant a dark, poorly ventilated, unsanitary fire hazard of a building containing far more than three families. The term had further been refined by the addition to the language of such terms as "dumb-bell tenement" and "dark bedroom." Reformers who surveyed these tenements urged state and city legislators to strengthen city housing codes. Jacob Riis, for example, has received credit for the passage of the laws outlawing the "dark bedroom." In *A Ten Years' War* he wrote of his visit to a rear tenement that had no windows to give it light or air: "In one big bed we counted six people, the parents and four children. Two of them lay crosswise at the foot of the bed, or there would not have been room."

Reform and the City's Children
In looking at the issue of housing, reformers focused particularly on the conditions under which children were forced to live. The emphasis on the welfare of children

is very clear throughout Riis's writings on New York City, but it was equally present in the works of reporters from other areas. For example, an observer of the Chicago urban scene wrote: "Little idea can be given of the filth and rotten tenements, the dingy courts and tumble-down sheds, the foul stables and dilapidated outhouses, the broken sewer pipes, the piles of garbage fairly alive with diseased odors, and of the number of children filling every nook, working and playing in every room, eating and sleeping in every window sill, pouring in and out of every door, and seeming literally to pave every scrap of 'yard.' "

It is not surprising that reports of this kind centered on the conditions under which children had to live and play. The turn of the century was an optimistic age, buoyed by industrial growth to a position of endless belief in America's future. In the children of the nation rested that future. If they could not be saved, if urbanization blighted their lives, then industrialism had failed.

In *The Bitter Cry of the Children* John Spargo recounted some of the most painful stories of the lives of urban children. His particular concern was the plight of the children forced by economic necessity to work in the factories of the industrial city. Spargo knew that children in rural areas always had been asked to do their share of farm work, but he felt that the kinds of work done by children in cities was an entirely different matter. As he explained in 1906:

> Children have always worked, but it is only since the reign of the machine that their work has been synonymous with slavery. Under the old form of simple, domestic industry the very young children were assigned their share of work in the family. But this form of child labor was a good

and wholesome thing . . . child training in the
noblest and best sense. . . . But with the coming of the machine age all this was changed. . . .
In place of parental interest and affection there
was the harsh, pitiless authority of an employer
or his agent, looking, not to the child's well-being
and skill . . . but to the supplying of a great,
ever widening market for cash gain. . . . According to the census of 1900 there were . . .
1,752,187 children under sixteen years of age
employed in gainful occupation.

Reports like this one of Spargo's led to legislation restricting the hours and types of child labor, enforcing
compulsory attendance at school, and providing for
health and safety regulations in those industries where
child labor was permitted.

Progressivism and Urban Reform
Riis, Spargo, and their fellow writers of the 1890s and
1910s were the spokespeople for the great urban reform movement that would come to be known as pro-
gressivism. The Progressive movement, the most comprehensive reform movement of the early twentieth
century, would capture the imagination of an entire
generation of upper-middle-class, white, urban Americans. Without the attention of this group of people the
reporters who uncovered the evils of the city would have
had little success in their campaigns to clean up the city.

An important force in the new examination of the
city was the Protestant Church. With the influx of immigrants in the last two decades of the nineteenth century and the beginning exodus of the upper-middle and
upper classes to the suburbs, Protestant churches had
been losing their urban congregations. The last de-

cades of the nineteenth century and the first decades of the twentieth century marked the beginning of interdenominational Protestant cooperation around a theme that came to be called the "Social Gospel."

The Social Gospel was articulated most clearly by the Reverend Washington Gladden who characterized urbanization as "the force which gathers men into cities." In sermons and essays he questioned whether or not "equipping [the force] with steam and electricity" had not "created [a power] which was stronger than the intelligence which seeks to control it." In spite of this seeming pessimism in the face of urbanization, Gladden formulated a positive, optimistic theology that called for all Christians to work actively to help relieve the poverty of others.

Walter Rauschenbusch was a young minister who took up this call and carried it even further than Gladden had. Rauschenbusch believed that the living conditions of modern society, not innate ethnic or religious weakness, had created the masses of poor who were present in early twentieth-century cities. A typical response to the Social Gospel was the establishment of the Fresh Air Fund by the Reverend Willard Parsons. The Salvation Army was another example of an urban Protestant group formed to help the poor in cities.

A striking characteristic of the Progressive reform movement was the widespread presence of women among the ranks of the reformers. Perhaps the most famous of those was Jane Addams, who in 1889 established Hull House in Chicago. Hull House was not the first settlement house, but it was certainly the most famous. Patterned after Toynbee Hall, a settlement house that had been built in the slums of East London in 1884, Hull House and others like it were community centers located in slums. The settlement workers were for the most part educated women who built recreational facilities for children, taught classes in English, the arts, and home economics to women, and provided meals for those who needed them.

The settlement house workers continued the Progressive era work of studying and writing about urban conditions. In her memoirs a settlement house worker, Agnes Sinclair Holbrook, described the Chicago slums around Hull House:

> . . . between Polk and Erving Streets, and also between Erving and Forquer, where there are no alleys, the condition of the rear tenements is the most serious. It is customary for the lower floor of the rear houses to be used as a stable and outhouse, while the upper rooms serve entire families as a place for eating, sleeping, being born and dying. . . . People are noticeably undersized and unhealthy, as well to the average observer as to the trained eye of the physician. Especially do the many workers in the tailoring trade look dwarfed and ill-fed; they walk with a peculiar stooping gait, and their narrow chests and cramped hands are unmistakable evidence of their calling. TB prevails, especially in diseases of the lungs and intestines, and deformity is not unusual. The mortality among children is great, and the many babies look starved.

Into conditions like these moved women like Jane Addams, Vida Scudder, and Lillian Wald. There were one hundred settlements by 1900 and four hundred in 1910. The settlement houses were more than community centers and more than focal points from which to study urban society. They were part of a Progressive attack on the problems of urban America, and their very existence was a testimony to the optimistic Progressive belief that change could be effected among the most desperate of the city's poor. As Addams herself said in *Twenty Years at Hull-House*, "[The settlement house] is an experimental effort to aid in the solution of the social and industrial problems engendered by the modern conditions of life. It is an attempt to relieve, at the same time, the overaccumulation at one end of society and the destitution at the other."

Moral Reform: The City
as the Root of Social Evil
The optimism and positive attitude of the Progressive reformers, coupled with their white Protestant upper-middle-class origins, caused them to attack conditions they considered to be social ills as well as conditions of poverty, disease, and corruption. From Riis to Addams, these reformers worked as hard to remove saloons and prostitution from the cities as they did to remove tenements and slums.

The liquor business, known as the "liquor interest," had long been associated with vice and the corruption of the honest workingman. By the early twentieth century the widespread presence of saloons in all of the nation's cities led reformers to believe that liquor was at the root of much of the crime and poverty they witnessed. Eradicate the saloon, they believed, and many of the city's problems could be solved.

An article in a Chicago newspaper connected saloons to gambling and prostitution. Writing in 1900, the reporter noted, "the laboring men and boys of Chicago find in the saloon . . . things which appeal to their lowest natures. Almost without exception the saloons exhibit pictures of the nude . . . gambling is open and

unrestricted, whenever sufficient 'hush money' is paid
. . . the social vice [prostitution] flourishes in connection with the liquor traffic. The saloons have a dance-hall in the rear and a house of ill-fame above all under one management."

The irony of this moral reform movement was that it met its greatest success in the rural areas. Men like William Jennings Bryan who feared the disappearance of an older agricultural America stood strongly behind the Prohibition movement. Liquor to Bryan was another example of the city's evils. His supporters felt the same, but they were scattered throughout rural areas and were no match for the municipal conglomerate of workingmen, police, politicians, and liquor. The population that came to live in "dry" states in the early years of the twentieth century was overwhelmingly rural.

The Progressive moral reformers won greater support for their stand against prostitution. Unlike the saloons, prostitution found no public defenders. Reformers connected the rising numbers of prostitutes to the terrible working conditions and low wages endured by women, particularly immigrant women, in the cities. As with other types of Progressive reform, the subject was scrutinized, and municipal commissions were formed to study the problem. A report published in Chicago in 1911 found the immigrant girl to be the source of urban prostitution because of the "lack of adequate protection and assistance given her after she reaches the United States" and the low wages that drove her to an occupation that promised riches.

The moral reformers sought solutions to prostitution in crackdowns on police corruption and recommendations for higher wages for men so that their wives and daughters would not be forced onto the streets. They did not favor sex education; as one report noted, "intelligence regarding sexual matters, if dictated by moral sentiment, is a safeguard to the youth of the community . . . the indiscriminate circulation of sexual information among children by means of books and pamphlets suggests a danger which ought not to escape attention."

Whether the reformers focused on prostitution, liquor and saloons, tenements, political corruption, labor conditions, or the rights of children, the underlying enemy was the city. Industrialism, immigration, and urbanization had exploded the agricultural society that was central to the American experience from 1620 until the second half of the nineteenth century. These reformers liked much of what they saw in the new American cities, and they believed that they could cure the rest. In their search for solutions they shed forever a belief that private charity was the answer for urban problems affecting thousands of lives. They began the movement toward formal social legislation that would be a trademark of city and state governments during the rest of the twentieth century. Along with this came the sense that legislation—as in the case of child labor—must be preventive. As a settlement house worker, Josephine Shaw Lowell, expressed it in a report to a New York City commission, "If the working people [in the cities] had all they ought to have, we should not have the paupers and the criminals. It is better to save them before they go under than to spend your life fishing them out when they're half-drowned, and taking care of them afterwards."

By the time of World War I the process of urbanization was, in a sense, complete. Industrialism had transformed the size and shape of the cities. Immigration had determined the character of the urban population. And reformers had revealed urban problems and suggested solutions to problems that would be studied and tried again and again in the twentieth century.

7

1920: Watershed Year and After

Most years in history can be claimed by one movement or another as a watershed, a turning point. Often these dates are questioned, and historians argue the merits of one over another as the dividing line for this movement or that one. For example, was 1620 (the date the Pilgrims arrived in New England) or 1776 (the opening year of the American Revolution) the turning point in the growth of democracy?

World War I and Urban Growth
There can be little argument, however, about the central importance of the date 1920 in any history of American urbanization. The federal census taken in that year revealed that for the first time urban-dwellers outnumbered those American citizens living in rural areas. In that year 5.4 million people were counted as urbanites, 5.1 million as farm dwellers. Of even greater importance were the statistics that pointed to a new stage in urban development—the growth and spread of the metropolis.

Metropolitan centers had first been identified in the census of 1910. These were cities that had considerable population in their central area (two hundred thousand) and an additional population density in surrounding areas. (These surrounding areas were universally called suburbs by the 1920s.) By the time of the census of 1920, there were fifty-eight metropolises. Two-thirds of the nation's total population (which had passed 100 million by 1920) lived in these metropolitan centers.

The boom in metropolitan growth between the 1910 census and 1920 census had many sources. First, as we have seen, the nation had been moving inexorably in the direction of its cities since the earliest years. World War I (1914–1918) brought a great influx of southern black people from rural areas of the South to the cities of the North. In 1910 Blacks accounted for only 2.5 percent of the entire northern urban population; by 1920 one-third of all black Americans lived in urban areas. In New York City alone the black population jumped from 91,000 in 1910 to over 150,000 a decade later. By 1930 more than five hundred thousand Blacks had left the South for northern cities. By 1930 Harlem was the most populous black area in the United States.

The end of World War I brought about other changes that greatly affected the growth of the new metropolitan urban areas. During the war immigration had slowed down. The peasants of the Austro-Hungarian and German empires were forced into their countries' armies and were not free to emigrate. Wartime conditions had made travel difficult and hazardous. With the end of the war, however, immigration soared almost to its prewar levels. Once again the immigrants flocked to America's cities. Along with them came thousands of American doughboys, World War I soldiers who had seen London and Paris and wanted to live in an urban environment.

The cities that attracted these two groups of people included both the older industrial city and a newer type of city whose economy was not basically industrial in nature but instead rested on recreation and leisure. Because of their climates Los Angeles and Miami both leaped into the front ranks of the metropolises in the 1920s. The growth of Los Angeles was most spectacular. In addition to its climate—or perhaps because of it—Los Angeles became home to the new movie industry. Between 1920 and 1930 Los Angeles would stand among the top three cities of the nation in terms of the rapidity of its population growth.

Automobiles and Urban Growth

Another facet of Los Angeles' growth that marked a new stage in the urbanization process was its immediate development as an automobile city. From the first the boundaries of this metropolitan center were determined by its roadways. The Federal-Aid Highway Act of 1916 had an enormous impact on the design of cities such as Los Angeles that grew after the invention of the automobile. Because of the spiderweb pattern of highways crisscrossing the area, Los Angeles never developed an inner city—a central area that decayed as newer areas of the city opened up—in the same way that older eastern cities had.

However, the automobile affected the growth of older cities too. Industries such as oil and automobile manufacturing and subsidiary companies such as tire producers attracted new workers to the cities where they were located. Houston, Texas, Oklahoma City and Tulsa, Oklahoma, Akron, Ohio, and Detroit, Michigan all mushroomed into metropolitan areas under the impetus of the new car industry and its affiliated industries.

Most of the new metropolitan areas had large populations that were not engaged in factory work, because a characteristic of this stage of urban development was the growth of service industries. During the decade after 1920, wages and earning power rose significantly. This increase in the standard of living was accompanied by a diversification of the businesses and services available to city inhabitants. As Blake McKelvey noted in *The Emergence of Metropolitan America*, "the cities, especially the great metropolises, were better able to sustain the commercial, civic and cultural functions that characterized the great central cities. These activities include the huge department stores and specialty shops, the banks and hotels and restaurants, the towering office blocks and civic administrative clusters, the theatres and museums and galleries, all of which competed for downtown space, as well as the parks and zoos and public and private sports arenas and other resorts that clustered around the outskirts of the affluent cities." In short the new metropolis was marked by a great number of people employed outside those industrial factories that had been characteristic of the nineteenth-century industrial city.

The Beginnings of Suburbia
Perhaps the single most important trend in the urbanization of the country after 1920 was the expansion of the city into suburbia. It was, after all, the addition of suburban satellites that gave rise to the term *metropolitan*. Where once cities had been surrounded by small villages that were distinctly rural in character, they now adjoined suburban towns that had little identity of their own and existed primarily as residential communities for people who worked in the businesses of the central city.

The automobile created this kind of suburb. When the decade of the 1920s opened, there were about eight million automobiles registered in the United States. At the close of the decade almost 25 million Americans had registered automobiles. These car owners thought nothing of a daily commute from homes in the new suburbs to work in the older districts of the cities. This life-style would set a pattern for urban outgrowth that would remain through the 1960s. In the 1920s, however, enough newcomers continued to pour into the

The sameness of suburbia at its extreme—
Levittown, Long Island, in 1954

urban centers so that these areas experienced no decline in population. The movement to the suburbs was not yet seen as escapist "flight" from the crime and dirt of the older inner cities. Instead, many cities pushed into suburban areas as a way to relieve overcrowding. Their boosters and promoters were proud of the ensuing spread into the countryside.

The growth of the suburb stimulated a fear among some observers that the new metropolitan areas were losing their distinctive flavor, that each city and each suburb was too much like the next. The fear that the city meant the regimentation of life would be a constant cry from 1920 onward. Houses looked alike in the suburbs, and people traveled to and from work in the cities on the same trains at the same times. Suburbs seemed synonymous with conformity.

The Artist and the City
If the suburbs seemed to herald a bland sameness for the metropolises of the 1920s, the inner city was experiencing one of its greatest surges of artistic interest and creative energy. For the first time since the founding of the nation, a sizable group of the nation's intellectual leaders not only lived in cities but praised those cities. As Lewis Mumford, one of the leading historians and sociologists of the city, noted in *The City in History*, "With the beginning of the second decade of this century, there is some evidence of an attempt to make a genuine culture out of industrialism," and by industrialism Mumford meant also urbanism.

The "attempt to make a genuine culture" included the establishment of artists' colonies in all major metropolitan areas. Places like Greenwich Village in New York blossomed after 1920. Soon every metropolis would have its own cultural and intellectual center where art, music, and literature of a distinctly urban flavor would be produced. With the revolution in communications wrought by the coming of movies and radio, the products of the media would be spread widely throughout the nation and would add to the aura and lure of the great metropolitan areas. If the census of 1920 had left any doubts of the city's superiority over the country, the airwaves and movie screens removed them.

The Great Depression and the City

The city's dominance of the American scene after 1920 meant that the triumphs of the metropolis—its prosperity, its cultural innovation, its trend-setting fashions—would be the triumphs of the nation. On the other hand, the failures of the metropolitan area would also send shock waves through the nation. This was painfully clear in the 1930s, the years of America's Great Depression.

The stock market crash of October 1929 occurred, of course, in the nation's largest city, New York. What was most important for other metropolises was the realization that they were connected financially to the fate of the stock market in New York. Boston, Philadelphia, Chicago, St. Louis, Kansas City, Atlanta, San Francisco, and many more of the new metropolitan centers were immediately shaken by the financial collapse in New York. As big businessmen in these cities attempted to constrict their businesses and cut their losses, millions of workers were expelled from their jobs. A great percentage of these unemployed lived in cities.

The presence of these needy people galvanized many municipal governments into shouldering unprecedented aid programs. Some kind of municipal responsibility for the poor and unemployed had long been a practice in American cities. However, as would also be the case with state and federal programs, the demands of the Great Depression brought into being a far wider system of municipal aid. The machinery of these programs would remain in place long after the Depression had ended and would characterize the metropolises well into the second half of the twentieth century.

For example, long before Franklin Roosevelt's New Deal created work for the unemployed, seventy-five cities had spent more than $420 million on public work projects. Monopoly® players will recognize the term Community Chest. The original Community Chest, however, was a national municipal network designed to provide aid for the poor and unemployed. For the inhabitants of American cities during the Depression, the bonuses from the Community Chest were real and all too necessary.

The Depression brought about a new relationship between the city and the federal government. Until the 1930s urban areas had looked to their state governments for funding. In many states, because of population distribution, the cities dominated the state legislatures. In many others, however, the distribution of representatives and public sentiment that favored rural America combined to block state aid to municipalities. In the face of the crushing needs of their citizens during the Depression, the metropolises could not afford to wait for the farm blocs to relinquish their stranglehold on state legislatures.

Spurred by rising unemployment and desperate poverty, the mayors of many major metropolitan areas turned to the federal government for aid. Mayor James Curley of Boston and Jimmy Walker of New York appealed to President Herbert Hoover rather than their state legislatures to alleviate the problems of their

Depression-torn cities. New groups of social workers took up the work in the cities that the settlement houses had carried on before the war. At this point, however, rather than appeal to the states for aid, these groups of reformers appealed to the federal government. Urbanization after 1920 was a national phenomenon; by 1930 the problems of urbanization could be dealt with only on a national scale. As one observer remarked in 1934, "The Federal Government is deeply concerned with housing and city planning, with child welfare, with the problems of commerce and labor." These were the same problems that the Progressives had addressed through city and state governments in the prewar years. Now magnified by the lens of the metropolis, these proved fit problems for the machinery of federal government.

The Works Progress Administration (WPA) is perhaps the best example of the sensitivity shown by the federal government to the needs of the metropolitan areas during these years. Under the WPA, federal jobs were created for artists, playwrights, actors, writers, and many others, all of whom were part of the metropolitan scene. The Federal Music Project, for example, served a dual role for a metropolis. On the one hand, the agency provided jobs for out-of-work musicians. On the other hand, the musicians provided entertainment for thousands of poverty-stricken unemployed people in the central cities. Fiorello LaGuardia, mayor of New York, returned again and again to the federal government for funds to help him relieve unemployment in his city. He eventually gathered more than $500 million in New Deal funds, some of which went toward the construction of a complex highway system that would help New York, already the nation's leading metropolis, expand even further.

The City in National Politics

The new relationship between the metropolis and the national government had important implications for politics. The election of Franklin Roosevelt as president in both 1932 and 1936 demonstrated the importance of the big-city vote. Roosevelt captured the majority in such cities as New York, Detroit, Boston, and Chicago. Winning in these metropolitan areas meant winning the electoral votes of the states in which they were located. The cities had captured the popular imagination in the 1920s; by the 1930s they dominated the political imagination as well.

On the local scene cities were beginning to rethink their form of organization. As they established their autonomy from state governments and worked to negotiate as individual bodies with the federal government, it was necessary for metropolitan areas to define themselves and to find some way to organize the central city with the suburban area surrounding it. Communications improvements allowed the radio stations and newspapers of the central city to influence a wide area. Services such as water, gas, and electricity had to be provided to the outlying areas of the metropolis.

By the middle of the 1930s it was clear to many observers that the best form of municipal organization for the large metropolitan areas was the "metropolitan county charter," which would consolidate the services necessary for the central city and the outlying suburbs. In the course of this reorganization both county and federal governments in the larger urban areas assumed tasks that had been the responsibility of the older industrial cities.

On the eve of World War II the United States was overwhelmingly urban. Yet the outbreak of this second world war brought another great surge of people into the nation's cities. Housing shortages replaced the job shortages of the 1930s as workers rushed to fill spots created in wartime industries. The metropolis into which they swarmed was the legacy of the prosperity of the 1920s and the hardships of the 1930s. The cries of economic breakdown and now world war had prevented Americans from taking a very long look at the everyday problems of life in the great metropolises. This would have to wait until the victory over Germany and Japan.

8

Modern Cities: Problems and Promises

In 1950 the Bureau of the Census invented yet another new term to help account for the living patterns of urban Americans. The Standard Metropolitan Statistical Area (SMSA) defined urban areas where a central city of fifty thousand or more inhabitants, together with the people living around that center, formed "an integrated economic and social unit with a large population nucleus." The new category signaled two movements in the ongoing process of American urbanization: first, the tendency of urban areas to sprawl outside their original boundaries in such complex ways that it was impossible to define exactly what the boundaries of any given city might be; and second, the exodus of people from the central city to the outlying suburbs, which had been in progress since the end of World War II and would continue with ever-increasing speed in the 1950s, 1960s, and 1970s. In fact, by 1970, when two-thirds of the nation lived in SMSAs, most of these urbanites lived outside the center city (an area that in the 1960s came to be called the "inner city," usually in a negative way).

Transportation and the Modern City
This step in the urbanization process, like so many that had gone before it, was directly tied to a revolution in transportation. In this case the automobile was the agent of change. With the end of World War II, with its rationing of rubber and gasoline, there was a major boom in car sales. Families could locate in suburbs that were as many as fifty miles from urban places where the families' breadwinners worked, and those breadwin-

ners could still expect to be at work within a reasonable commuting time.

By the late 1950s "reasonable" commuting time was already a topic of heated debate. But no matter how badly American drivers became snarled in traffic jams, car ownership soared in the years between 1945 and 1960. By 1957 over 60 percent of all people commuting to the downtown business districts in a majority of the nation's largest cities used private automobiles to get there. (In this pattern of commuting traffic New York, for once, was atypical of the nation as a whole. Residents of that city continued to rely overwhelmingly on mass transit to get to work.) At the same time that more people were commuting from the suburbs to the city in private cars, the demand on mass transit declined sharply. Because of this shift in consumer taste in transportation the cities and the federal government joined forces to build miles and miles of new highways while they allowed the mass transit systems within the cities to deteriorate.

Los Angeles is undoubtedly the most striking example of a modern city with no center, a sprawling "megalopolis" where commuting many miles by car is a way of life for most of the city's inhabitants. In fact, Los Angeles is so unfocused that it has been jokingly referred to as "suburbs in search of a city." Los Angeles has come under attack as the epitome of the kind of city whose citizens are removed from the city. Although this may be true on a larger scale for Los Angeles than for other cities, it was certainly true of all modern cities that they seemed in the 1960s and 1970s to have lost their focus. As Daniel J. Boorstin has written in *The Americans: The National Experience,* "Highways built to serve only the automobile were insulated

from the landscape, from pedestrians and from people going about their business. The separated highway, on which more and more Americans would spend more and more of their waking hours, isolated citizens from one another and from their city."

The Deterioration of the Inner City
The development of the highway and the dominance of the automobile on the American landscape might well be mourned on Boorstin's terms. Yet there was a greater evil attendant on the automobile's onslaught on American cities. As attention and funding turned to the outer edges of the urban areas, the inner city disintegrated even further. Only the relatively wealthy drove cars and lived in suburbs. Victims of poverty and discrimination were left behind. Where once the middle and upper classes had shared geographical space with less fortunate citizens of the city and—as was certainly true in the Progressive era—were frequently stimulated to aid the needy they saw around them, those who fled to the suburbs could close their eyes to the conditions they left behind.

Indifference thus joined hands with progress to create the "inner city" of the second half of the twentieth century. To most observers, "inner city" was rapidly becoming synonymous with black ghettos. By 1960 nearly three-quarters of all black Americans lived in cities. Discrimination and lack of equal economic opportunity kept black Americans from moving out of the city. At the same time, funding priorities were focused on

Leading the nation in suburban sprawl is Los Angeles

roads to the suburbs, not on the mass transportation system that the poorer workers needed to get from the ghetto to their jobs.

Disinterested white suburbanites pointed out that slums had always been a part of the urban landscape, particularly in the inner city. However, the older slums that had been studied by the reformers at the turn of the century were peopled with immigrant groups who had reason to believe that hard work and the passage of time would lead them to a better life in the city. This hope was missing for black Americans who, because of discrimination based on skin color, knew that hard work did not lead to a promotion and who, until the 1970s, knew that the homes of suburbia were closed to them regardless of their incomes.

Despair led in Harlem to a pattern that Gilbert Osofsky, in his study of that area, *Harlem: The Making of a Ghetto*, has called "the cycle of decay." Harlem is the most important black enclave in the nation, both in terms of the numbers of its citizens and in terms of its place in black social and intellectual history. Ironically, Harlem's best times came during eras of the harshest discrimination in northeastern cities. In the 1920s and 1930s there was nowhere for middle- and upper-middle-class black professionals to live except Harlem. While they remained in the area, they helped to keep Harlem prosperous. With the end of the 1960s and the successful legislative attack on many forms of discrimination, these middle- and upper-class black Americans fled to the suburbs too, leaving behind only those people who had no hope of leaving the ghettos.

In *Dark Ghetto* Kenneth B. Clark explains the hopelessness of the ghetto this way: "Ghettos are not viable communities. . . . [The ghetto] cannot support its people; most have to leave it for their daily jobs. Its businesses are geared toward the satisfaction of personal needs and are marginal to the economy of the city as a whole. The ghetto feeds upon itself; it does not produce goods or contribute to the prosperity of the city." The black—and Puerto Rican—ghettos are the misshapen late-twentieth-century grandchildren of the original workingmen's residential areas of the nineteenth-century city. The ghetto is the least attractive trait of modern urbanization, yet in many minds it is the thing that most characterizes the large modern city. Rehabilitation projects designed to clean up ghetto areas have repeatedly failed, destroyed by the violence and despair that characterize life in these areas. As Alfred Kazin has written in an article entitled "Fear of the City" (*American Heritage,* 1983), "Vast housing projects have become worse than the slums they replaced and regularly produce situations of peril for the inhabitants themselves. To the hosts of the uprooted and disordered in the city, hypnotized by the images of violence increasingly favored by the media, the city is nothing but a state of war."

Controversy over the
Future of the Inner City
Many urban historians, among them Richard Wade, are optimistic about the future of large cities, in spite of the reality of conditions as Kazin explains them. Wade has argued that violence and race conflict are longtime parts of the American urban tradition, and he believes, as he put it in a 1979 *American Heritage* article, that "American cities are (mostly) better than ever." He cites a variety of statistics to support his claim. Although it is sometimes difficult to compare economic statistics from

one era to the next, by the criteria of their times city officials in 1902 found that over half the population in urban areas lived below the poverty line. In 1970 those urbanites who lived below the poverty line accounted for only a fifth of the urban population as a whole.

When Jacob Riis surveyed tenement conditions at the turn of the century, he estimated that in the Tenth Ward in New York City, more than three hundred thousand people were crowded into each square mile. In today's city more than seventy-five thousand people per square mile is officially considered to be "intolerable." Wade also has examined the city schools that were so highly prized by the immigrants of the nineteenth century, and again he finds conditions wanting. One of the goals of the urban educational reformers in the early twentieth century was to reduce the numbers of students in elementary classrooms to fifty! Certainly it would be hard to argue that early urban classrooms were as healthy, well lighted, or well staffed as schools today, nor did they offer such an imaginative range of courses.

Whether the cities improved or declined in real terms over the course of the three decades following the end of World War II, it was certainly the perception of most Americans that the trend was a downward one. A typical article of the late 1960s detailed as "normal" the following criminal activity in one of Chicago's city precincts: "365 crimes . . . including 86 reported burglaries . . . 33 reported car thefts . . . 43 reported assaults . . . nine reported robberies. . . . There was a murder and two attempted rapes. . . . On seven occasions the police made vice arrests, five times for narcotics violations, once for gambling and once for prostitution." To the article's readers in suburbia this kind of report was more reason for staying in the safer, if culturally less exciting, world of the suburb.

Unemployment,
Race Relations, and the City

By the late 1960s another trend had been noted in the inner city. Unemployed Americans living in these areas had begun to stop looking for work. By 1970 about 75 percent of all black American males were counted in the work force of the country; that is, they were either employed or looking for employment. In Watts, a ghetto area of Los Angeles that typified other ghettos at this time, slightly over half of the black male population could be counted as being in the work force. Over the course of the decade of the 1960s almost 15 percent of the black male citizens of Watts had simply stopped looking for jobs that they felt would never materialize.

In addition to the growing despair and mental anguish felt by these men, there was a continuing decline of the area and a spiraling deterioration of its buildings and businesses. By 1970, urbanization, for the first time in America, meant that a significant portion of the population in densely populated areas of cities lived without hope of improvement and, seeing no future for themselves, worked toward no future goals for their urban homes. This urban crisis of the 1960s, as the explosive race riots of that decade proved, was a crisis of race relations. Throughout the decade black Americans in Watts, Harlem, the South Side of Chicago, and a host of lesser-known ghettos destroyed the property in these areas to show their frustration with the deteriorating conditions where they lived.

As Nathan Glazer wrote in 1970 in *Cities in Trouble,*

Almost every urban problem in the United States has a racial dimension, and the racial dimension in almost every problem is the key factor. . . . When we consider transportation, for example, we discover that Negroes are more dependent on public transportation, and their housing is more seriously affected by urban freeway construction. When we consider all the problems of urban adjustment, we find higher rates of family breakup, illegitimacy, crime and illness—mental and physical—among Negroes. When we consider problems of urban government, we find that its chief issues are affected by the racial crisis. If people are for extending the governments of cities to include suburban areas, it will be because more affluent whites will provide more taxes for city services, which it is hoped will benefit the black poor.

During the administrations of John F. Kennedy and Lyndon B. Johnson, billions of dollars were poured into cities, a new department of the cabinet was formed to deal with urban issues, and yet the problems mounted. American cities seemed to have come finally to the point that Wendell Phillips, a New England minister, had predicted more than a century before. He had preached that "the time will come when our cities will strain our institutions as slavery never did."

The 1980s:
Change, Hope, and Growth
Yet by 1980, although conditions in the inner city were still intolerable, there was a perceptible change of mood where the city was concerned. Although unemployment in the inner city was still far higher than that of the nation as a whole, and the gap between black and white wage earners was still intolerably wide, the city was no longer referred to as "crumbling," "in crisis," or "doomed." The city of 1980 suffered from housing

shortages, fiscal crises, and deathly pollution problems—all old familiar tunes in the repertoire of industrial urbanization. What the 1980 city did not lack was
hope and youth.

Youthful politicians of all races held mayoralty seats,
claimed a love for their cities, and believed in their fu-
tures. Young men and women who had grown up in
the suburbs of the 1950s and 1960s were moving into
the city to live, reclaiming dilapidated neighborhoods
and infusing new energy into the city's culture. The
process of turning a once dilapidated neighborhood into
a comfortable residential area is called gentrification.
When this happens, however positive the change for
the city, there are some negative effects. People with
low incomes are often forced from the neighborhood
because gentrification is usually accompanied by rising
rents.

The new urban-dwellers were in some ways remi-
niscent of the Progressive reformers at the turn of the
century. In important ways they were different. These
were not upper-class society youth who had seen their
genteel world assaulted by industrialism and immigration. Instead, these were the grandchildren of immigrants. Their parents and grandparents had followed the
path that meant prosperity in the process of urbanization—moving from immigrant ghettos to residential
areas of the city and from there to the suburbs.

The cities they are creating in the 1980s are truly
pluralistic. Racial, ethnic, and religious barriers as their
ancestors had known them are not a part of their urban world. Social standing based on money and occupation is. So is a determination to improve the quality
of life in the city for all—through support of cultural
institutions, the refurbishing of public schools and libraries, the renovation of city architecture, and new efforts at pollution control. The 1980s successor to the

frontier booster is the city magazine. Each major metropolitan area has one. Places like New York, San Francisco, Chicago, Atlanta, and even smaller cities publish slick, attractive journals that focus on the benefits of downtown living.

Besides this movement into the city by young, promising professionals, there has been another significant change in the process of urbanization in the decade or so since 1970. As sociologists point out, there are two basic patterns in the urban development of any nation, and from 1790 to 1970 the United States exhibited both of these. First, the population of established cities grows faster than the population of the nation as a whole, and second, a number of rural areas expand rapidly enough to become urban in character. In the United States between 1970 and 1980 this first condition ceased. For the first time cities did not grow faster than the nation as a whole. And in the northeastern, most highly urbanized states, the second trend also stopped. For the first time since 1790, no new rural areas became urban, according to the census of 1980. The inner cities during this decade maintained about the same population, but a major shift occurred when people moved in large numbers from older "inner suburbs" to outer suburbs. The result of this shifting is further urban sprawl. In highly urbanized areas such as the Atlantic coast from Boston to Washington, D.C., the cities have melted together into a huge supercity, but the population seems to be shifting within the established boundaries of this area. In other words small towns in rural Vermont and New Hampshire, western Massachusetts, and upstate New York are not being caught up in the process of urbanization.

How to measure what is urban remains a problem. There are, of course, the administrative boundaries of a city. Take, for example, all of the people in Boston who have the right to vote for the mayor of that city. Then, however, consider all of the people in the outlying suburbs of Boston, who do not vote for the mayor but consider themselves to be Bostonians. In an attempt to clarify the definition once again, the Census Bureau in 1980 defined the city as "any group of 50,000 people with an average density of 1,000 per square mile." By avoiding the terms *city* or *center city*, the Census Bureau reflected their awareness of the urban sprawl. By the new definition the same number of Americans, 58 percent, lived in "urbanized areas" in 1980 as had lived there in 1970. Applying the new definition to the statistics from other modern census reports, we find 46 percent of all Americans were living in urban areas in 1950 and 53 percent in 1960. Until the decade of the 1970s there had been only one other decade in American history when the urban population failed to increase. This was the decade of the 1810s, a decade that saw the doubling of the geographic land mass of the country through the purchase of the Louisiana Territory.

The figures from the census of 1980 indicate that the United States is embarking on a new stage in the process of urbanization. Some of the characteristics of this next stage are beginning to emerge. The amount of land that is urbanized is likely to increase even if the percentage of the population in urban areas remains the same. What this means is a greater distance from the inner city to the outer edges of the suburbs. The same number of people live in these areas, but the land inhabited by these urban-dwellers is much larger.

In most states the amount of land that is counted as urban is far less than the amount of territory considered to be rural. California is a good example of this.

In this state the census found 91 percent of the state's population living in urban areas, but 96 percent of the land in the state fell outside these areas. In spite of this disparity there were already signs that the land area was becoming urbanized at a rate much faster than the rate at which the population was continuing to urbanize. In California many of the cities are more densely populated than cities of similar size back East, and so the spreading of the urban population onto new land is probably inevitable. California cities do not seem as overcrowded as the cities of New York or Illinois or Pennsylvania, because in California, cities created by the automobile boom show a much less distinct break between the urban centers and the outlying suburbs.

Shifting Population
Finally, the census of 1980 revealed that southern and western urban areas still showed the two trends of growth in established cities and the development of new urban areas that had been the pattern of the rest of the country for so many years. What this means is that the South and West are still urbanizing in the traditional sense of the word. These are the "Sun Belt" areas that have attracted attention and population over the last decade.

The term *Sun Belt* generally refers to such states as Florida, Texas, Arizona, and California. During the decade of the 1970s the population in these areas swelled

Houston and other cities in the Sun Belt are currently undergoing the rapid growth of traditional urbanization.

immensely. Much of this population growth came from the migration of people to Sun Belt areas from the states in the northeastern and midwestern sections of the country. Cities like San Diego, Phoenix, Los Angeles, Dallas, and Houston grew tremendously. Houston alone doubled its population between 1960 and 1980. Overall, the population in western states rose 24 percent, and the population in southern states rose 20 percent in the 1970s.

Lower fuel costs, less pollution, and milder climates, as well as recent reforms in politics and social conditions, make these areas highly desirable locations for the establishment of new businesses and the relocation of old ones. Along with population growth has come increasing political power for these areas. Over the past decade, the Sun Belt states have gained almost twenty seats in Congress. There are some drawbacks to living in the Sun Belt, however. For one thing, many of these areas have limited water supplies, and compared to the cities of the Northeast they are far more likely to experience serious water shortages. In addition, some Sun Belt areas have fewer fuel resources than cities in the Northeast and Midwest.

Nevertheless, this southwestern shift of the population center is a major facet in the current chapter of urbanization. The people living in the Sun Belt tend to be younger, so there is likely to be a higher birth rate in this area for the next several years. Of the twenty-five largest cities, according to the census of 1980, twelve—all located in the Sun Belt—had gained population by 1982. Six other major cities lost population. All of the latter were located in the Northeast and Midwest, areas observers have come to call the "Frost Belt" or "Rust Bowl."

By 1980 there were twenty-nine supercities with a total population of 89 million people. Supercities are those metropolitan areas that include a central city, suburbs, and outer areas that have come to be called "exurbia." Towns in exurbia are small cities in and of themselves. People who live in exurbia tend to work there and infrequently make the lengthy trip to the inner city, even though they are considered to be part of that city's populace. New patterns of urbanization are emerging in these cities.

The city, which has always occupied a controversial position in American thought has survived the lowest point to date in its long history, the devastation and despair of the 1960s and 1970s. With the new decade of the 1980s has come a new optimism about the city and its future. More important, the new optimism has been accompanied by a move within urban areas from suburbs back to the city proper. At the same time, the overall growth of many of the nation's older urban areas has slowed. Without the pressure of the constantly increasing numbers that have been a central factor of urban life for centuries, it will perhaps be possible to assess the state of the cities and plan for the next stages in the country's urbanization.

9

Cities:
Past, Present, Future

In 1968 Edward Banfield published a widely acclaimed analysis of the urban crisis, *The Unheavenly City*. He took his title from a treatise by Cotton Mather, an early Puritan minister. Mather had written "Come hither, and I will show you an admirable Spectacle! 'Tis an Heavenly CITY. . . . A CITY to be inhabited by an innumerable Company of Angels, and by the Spirits of Just Men . . . O America, the Holy City."

By borrowing from Mather's words for the title for his book, Banfield demonstrated his recognition that the United States has been from the beginning an urban nation. Certainly the urbanization of the colonies was modest compared to that of the twentieth century, but for their times colonial cities were truly urban. In the nineteenth century, as America took the lead as both an industrial nation and as a haven for immigrants, urbanization accelerated. The United States became far more urban than the nations of Western Europe.

At the same time that this rapid expansion of American cities was taking place, however, the eyes of many Americans and foreign observers were focused on the uninhabited expanses of the American continent, not on the cities where an increasing percentage of the American population lived.

Important as the wilderness is to any understanding of the American character, the history of urbanization in the United States is at least as important as the history of the frontier. And since the frontier as the pioneers knew it vanished nearly a century ago, a strong case could be made that ultimately urbanization will outweigh the wilderness in importance.

From the time of the census of 1920 the United States has been statistically an urban nation. For much of the twentieth century, urban living has been the characteristic way of life for a majority of American citizens. By 1980, 170 million people in the United States lived in urban areas. There were twenty-five cities in the country that contained more than 450,000 people. One hundred American cities had a population greater than 150,000. These cities were spread across the continent throughout the fifty states. They included Honolulu and Cleveland, Houston and Seattle, Milwaukee and Jacksonville. New York was still the largest, but Los Angeles was fast gaining on the front-runner.

Critics of the big cities of the 1980s argue that the megalopolis has destroyed the individual characteristics that made New Orleans distinct from Charleston and Boston different from Philadelphia. The supercities all seem alike. They are each surrounded by a network of highways dotted with green interstate markers. Chain retail stores, from Burger King and McDonald's to Sears and K Mart, make shopping in one city not unlike shopping in any other. Mass-media announcers have done their best to erase regional accents.

Yet for the citizens of these cities, living in one city is very different from living in another. Life in Baltimore is different from life in St. Paul, Minnesota, and not just because of the climate. A new civic pride has infused the city dwellers of the 1980s. This civic pride often manifests itself in restoration and preservation projects designed to save the heritage and character of individual cities. In spite of the sameness that the technological world has stamped on many parts of the city, there will always be neighborhoods of shops and buildings that reflect the unique flavor of a city's background and development.

Between the mid-1980s and the year 2000 the cities must find solutions to a host of serious problems: pollution, fiscal disorder, and the continuing presence of an underemployed, despairing minority population. Finding the solutions to these problems will undoubtedly alter the urbanization process in ways that will be felt well into the twenty-first century. The President's Commission for a National Agenda for the 1980s, a bipartisan group appointed by President Carter, has already suggested a controversial solution to some of these problems in urging the federal government to spend money on programs that would encourage migration to Sun Belt cities, rather than spend the same funds to shore up the older cities of the Northeast. Population trends indicate that people are already moving in this direction. The rapid development of these new Sun Belt cities is also destined to change urbanization.

Whatever the changes, urban living is bound to remain a way of life for the majority of Americans. The city is noisy, dirty, and crime-ridden. It is also exciting, vital, and energetic. One hundred years ago Horatio Alger wrote of a boy's first visit to the city, "He walked about here and there, gazing with curious eyes at the streets and warehouses and passing vehicles, and thinking what a lively place New York was, and how different life was in the metropolis. . . . Somehow it seemed to wake [him] up and excite his ambition, to give him a sense of power which he had never felt before." More than any other force, urbanization has been fueled by this human attraction to the city. As long as there are people to be lured by the city's magic and power, urbanization will go on.

Suggestions for Further Reading

Urban history is a relatively new subject for historians. The problems in cities in the 1960s, particularly racial violence, stimulated historians to look for the roots of modern urbanization. Out of their search came many excellent books on urban history.

Several good, comprehensive surveys of American urban history have been written. Among these are *A History of Urban America* (third edition, 1983) by Charles Glaab and A. Theodore Brown and *The Rise of Urban America* (1965) by Constance M. Green. Two books that treat the critical period of the late nineteenth century, when the country was shifting from the farm to the city, are *The Age of Excess* (second edition, 1975) by Ray Ginger and *The Search for Order* (1967) by Robert Wiebe.

Certain specific topics in American history have been treated very well both by urban historians and by historians whose first interest was not the city but whose topic was closely connected to urbanization. An example of this latter category is Oscar Handlin's classic treatment of immigrants, *The Uprooted* (second edition, 1973). Other topics of special interest to students of urban history include transportation, covered by Sam Bass Warner, Jr., in *Streetcar Suburbs* (1962); race relations, detailed by Gilbert Osofsky in *Harlem: The Making of a Ghetto* (1966); and machine politics, the focus of Seymour Mandelbaum's *Boss Tweed's New York* (1965).

Several historians have compiled collections of documents that illuminate the city s past. Two examples of these are *The American City: A Documentary History* (1963), edited by Charles T. Glaab, and *City Life, 1865–1900: Views on Urban America* (1973), edited by Ann Cook, Marilyn Gittell, and Herb Mack.

For discussions of modern American cities and their future, readers should consult Sam Bass Warner, Jr., *The Urban Wilderness* (1972) and Edward C. Banfield, *The Unheavenly City Revisited* (1970 and paper edition, 1974).

Index